MODEL
RAILWAYS
ON A BUDGET

CYRIL FREEZER

A practical guide to inexpensive,
more enjoyable railway modelling.

D0517567

MODEL
RAILWAYS
ON A BUDGET

CYRIL FREEZER

Patrick Stephens
Wellingborough, Northamptonshire

First published in 1987

British Library Cataloguing in Publication Data

Freezer, C.J.
Model railways on a budget.
1. Railroads—Models
I. Title
625.1'9   TF197

ISBN 0-85059-821-4

Patrick Stephens Limited is part of the Thorsons Publishing Group,
Wellingborough, Northamptonshire, NN8 2RQ, England

Printed in Great Britain by Woolnough Bookbinding Limited,
Irthlingborough, Northamptonshire

3 5 7 9 10 8 6 4 2

CONTENTS

INTRODUCTION

This book has been written with one aim in mind, to help the reader avoid wasting his hard-earned money. Naturally, its main value will be for the impecunious, but I hope that some of the ideas I put forward may help those with a plentiful supply of cash to make better use of their resources.

Unfortunately, in what both the publishers and I see as a relatively small textbook, I have been unable to go into many constructional aspects in the depth I would like, and so I have added a bibliography to show where the interested modeller can look further for additional information on modelling techniques.

In writing the book I have received a great deal of help from a number of individuals, most of whom gave their assistance long before I switched on my word processor to start the text! In short, I am indebted to those who went before, and although I have made reference to many of them in the text, I feel it as well to list, strictly in alphabetical order, everyone who has, in one way or another, provided useful information and advice. As someone or other once said, if we can see further today, it is only because we are standing on the shoulders of giants.

To the following then, my thanks: John H. Ahern, for the 'Madder Valley' and all it meant to scenic modelling; Bill Banwell, for 'Maybank', arguably the first of the terminus-fiddle yard models; Edward Beal, for almost single-handedly launching 4 mm scale as a practical proposition; Maurice Deane, for branch line models in general, and 'Great Western' in particular; Peter Denny, for 'Buckingham' and friendship; Jack Dugdale, for reminding us that model railways are fun; Henry Greenly, for getting order out of chaos; G. P. (Percy) Keen, for the Model Railway Exhibition; Michael Longridge, for introducing me to quality modelling; S. A. Loxton (alias Precedent), for showing me the importance of prototype research; David Rowe, for 'Milkwood', and all that followed; E. W. Twining, for inspiration; A. R. Walkley, for pioneering the quality portable layout; Linn Westcott, for 'L' girder construction, and much else beside. Last of all, my son, Nick, for advice, proof-reading and criticism.

WORKING TO A BUDGET

There is a widespread belief that model railways are costly affairs. This is hardly surprising as the catalogue value of an established layout runs into hundreds of pounds. Yet railway modelling is actually one of the least expensive hobbies of all to pursue and can be enjoyed to the full on a shoe-string budget. The reason is quite elementary, almost all expenditure on the hobby is of a capital nature and running costs are negligible. Apart from this, the cost of a few magazines and a possible subscription to the local model railway club, the railway modeller need spend little other than on the acquisition of new models. There are some initial requirements but as they amount to little more than the contents of a good train set plus a power supply unit it is probable that the majority of readers of this book have something of the sort stuck in a cupboard. In practical terms, you can construct a high class model railway for very little indeed.

Nor does this low, almost negligible outlay limit you to a small, simple, low-grade model. I doubt if anyone would call Norman Eagles' 'Sherwood' or Peter Denny's 'Buckingham' small, simple or low grade — quite the reverse! Yet both were built to a strict budget, and although they now occupy large, purpose-built railway rooms, they began in a modest way many years ago.

I am not advocating any one specific scale or gauge, although through its wide availability 4 mm scale is generally the more economical and certainly the easiest to develop. All scales and gauges can be built on a budget since in practice, the main limitations on the model lie in the space available and the amount of time the builder can devote to his hobby. It is very easy to think that another scale or a different gauge would make all the difference. Believe me, it doesn't! So, if you happen to have a nucleus of a good layout in a decent, working train set, for heavens sake develop it before making a change. It is far better to stick to your initial gauge — remember that the layouts I have mentioned have been developed, on chosen themes, over a lifetime.

This is the key to economical railway modelling. A model railway, as opposed to a highly developed layout based on a commercial train set system, takes some considerable time to create. This is, of course, part of its attraction, the project is an ideal subject for a hobby, a completely open-ended undertaking which grows with the builder.

Rather more than 90 per cent of all you need to build a model

7

Above *Peter Denny's 'Buckingham' in its second phase, a portable layout housed in a small London flat in the 1950s. The line then represented a single track secondary branch, with a fairly sparse service, run by a small stud of scratchbuilt locos and a limited collection of rolling stock. All this was built up on a small weekly budget.*

railway can be produced in the home workshop from basic raw materials. Of course, this will take time, it certainly involves a degree of determination, and certainly implies the acquisition of some basic skills. This is the first hurdle the would-be modeller must leap. Almost anyone can make a model. Agreed, this implies the use of tools, but you have already learned how to use a knife and fork at table, and to write with a ballpoint pen or pencil. Because these skills are shared by almost everyone, we all tend to overlook the fact that they involve some very tricky manipulation. So, you *can* use tools!

Although you could, given a large enough workshop, make virtually everything yourself, there are several areas where it is advisable to use a commercial product. The first, and most important, is the area of low-voltage power supplies and the associated controllers. The second main area where some purchases are advisable, particularly in the smaller scales, is in the provision of locomotives, coaches and wagons. The truth is that the quality and price of current commercial items is such that you are hard pushed to equal, let alone improve on what is on offer in both quality and cost. Only where your master plan requires special prototypes need you consider making your own.

The third area where one ought to use commercial equipment is a more personal one. Whilst some of the ways of keeping within a budget I shall describe involve little more than careful planning, most exchange time for money, and this must never be forgotten. As I shall show later, constructing your own track is a straightfoward business, and, looking solely at material costs, saves money,

Below *Grandborough Junction on Peter Denny's 'Buckingham' line in the 1970s. The layout is now permanently erected in a large room in a Cornish vicarage, and has grown into a busy double track line with an intensive service. Again, everything in this photograph was built in the home workshop. The six-wheel coaches in this picture, which were the pride and joy of the line in the 1950s are now relegated to secondary services, and hauled by a model of a Sacre 'Altrincham' 2-4-0T.*

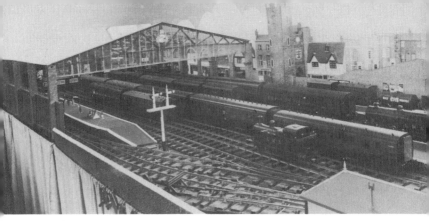

Above *Norman Eagles' 'Sherwood' line is one of the largest and most elaborate 0 gauge clockwork systems in the world. This photograph, taken in the line's sixtieth year of development, shows the main terminus, Nottingham Castle, a very elaborate affair as befits the principal station on a large, intensively operated network.*

Below *A view across a quarter of the 'Sherwood' lines, with Gretley Colliery dominating the middle ground. The model is in a large, purpose-built timber outbuilding, where it has been housed for nearly twenty years. Although this was costly, it was the culmination of a carefully thought out master plan, which has allowed Norman Eagles to enjoy his hobby, together with a group of good friends throughout a long and fruitful retirement. This is the ultimate end of sensible budgeting.*

providing we ignore the time involved. The idea of placing a charge against time spent on a hobby is, to many people, outrageous. In many hobbies, it is certainly pointless, but ours is the exception. Model railways are the largest and most complex of all models and we start where the others stop. A model railway only 2 metres long is extremely small, but a model airplane or model boat any bigger than this is exceptional. Furthermore, a good model railway involves its builder and creator in a wide range of modelling activities. If you don't happen to like one of these or, worse still, you aren't particularly good at it, then common sense suggests that you buy that part of the model and concentrate on the parts you enjoy and can do well.

Which brings me back to track. If you charge your time at £5 an hour — and that's very low indeed — then home-made track costs nearly three times the price of ready-assembled track, and pointwork is about 30 per cent more expensive. Worse is to come, for if your workmanship is suspect, and the track you build is so indifferent that the stock spends more time off it than on it, then

Alan Wright's 'Cheviotdale', a small 00 gauge layout based on North Eastern branch line practice, is a fine example of an economical system ideally suited for a limited budget. Although fitting into a tiny outhouse, the layout can be operated intensively in a realistic fashion, using only a handful of locomotives and rolling stock.

Martin Brent's 'Rye Harbour' was built to a tight budget, even though there was no need to economize. The underlying idea was to test techniques in EM gauge, with a view to establishing the best way to construct the main layout and there was no point in spending more than was absolutely essential. It was built in two stages, a small terminus, initially called 'Arcadia', then a harbour extension, transforming the layout and extending the operating potential. Once the layout had served its purpose, and been widely exhibited, it was sold (less rolling stock), making the entire process remarkably economical.

you're wasting both time and money. Personally, I see nothing wrong in wasting one or the other if that's your fancy, but to waste both at once is, at the very best, ridiculous! The point I want to make is that saving money isn't the main object of a budget, the idea is to spend what you have available to good purpose. And you do this the better if you also use your time to good purpose as well.

MATERIALS AND TOOLS

When one considers the price of the timber needed to construct a baseboard, it would be easy to believe that the stuff doesn't grow on trees after all! This highlights a fundamental problem — a model railway can use up a lot of basic raw materials, and as one would naturally prefer to spend the money on models instead, any means of saving hard cash in this area is very welcome. There are, of course, many occasions where it is advisable, if not absolutely essential, to buy raw materials, but there is no doubt that a lot of modelling can be undertaken using scrap, second-hand or otherwise discounted material.

Wood is an excellent case in point. As I said at the outset, bought from a timber merchant or DIY store it is fairly costly but there are other sources. Although one can no longer obtain good quality wooden cases from the grocers — supermarkets get their supplies in cardboard cartons these days — there are many other ways of getting hold of timber cheaply. A careful study of the local newspaper will show where the nearest firm offering second-hand builder's materials is situated. Providing you select the timber personally, and take care to see that it isn't afflicted with woodworm or dry rot and is free from obvious cracks and similar defects, this is

Probably the most useful saws for the modelmaker, the 6 in pin-ended hacksaw and razor saw.

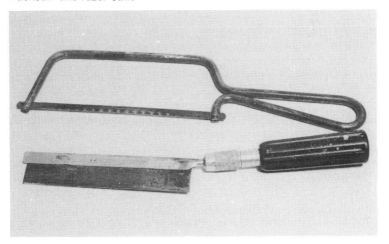

an excellent source of supply. The stuff is properly seasoned for one thing. Then, one can sometimes obtain offcuts of timber in varying sizes from small yards, or even off building sites.

Another source of raw material is packaging. For example, the stiff transparent plastic sheet found on many carded products is an ideal glazing material, and any flat sheets should be carefully put aside. I need hardly mention cardboard, this ranges from the stiff card used for packing cases to the thinner material employed for cartons. Cereal packets, for example, provide a quite useful source of modelling card, as do stiff office folders.

Plastics are often thrown away. Agreed, it's rather difficult to find flat sheets, though it isn't entirely impossible. Plastics are frequently formed into intricate shapes, and, as the space fantasy modellers have long known, these can be worked into interesting models. For our part, the potential of such items for industrial complexes is considerable.

Indeed, scrap of all sorts should be carefully considered. You can often salvage a quantity of useful metal rods from discarded equipment, not to mention numerous screws, nuts, washers and springs. It is true that a great deal of junk remains, obstinately, junk, long after the proverbial seven years is up, but this ought not to deter the economy-minded enthusiast from collecting sensibly.

Wire is a particularly useful material, and much can often be picked up for nothing. For example, the wire hanger, supplied by all dry cleaners, is a useful source of stiff steel wire. Copper wire, found in all scrap electrical cables, is also a versatile modelling material. The metal is very ductile — in other words, you can hammer it into shape — moreover, it can be straightened with comparative ease by stretching it to near breaking point.

It's all very well collecting a mass of bits and pieces, but if you don't store them properly, you'll never be able to find them. The 'junk box' is a pernicious item. Yes, you do need a couple of boxes into which you put items you think you might need someday, but I label mine 'SORT'. I've found that unless you put fittings into properly labelled boxes or drawers so that you can locate them easily when you need them, you might just as well throw them away for all the good they do.

Amass a collection of small rectangular tin boxes — the 2 oz tobacco tin is a traditional container, but anything is suitable. The plastic boxes that hold ice-cream are also very useful, indeed, there are more and more re-useable containers appearing every year. Save all the screw-top glass jars you can lay your hands on, up to

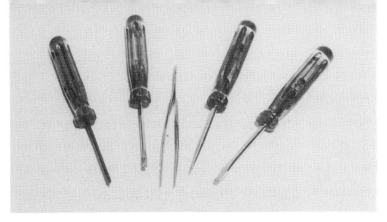

Top *A selection of small screwdrivers and a pair of tweezers—a useful kit for modelmaking.*

Above *From top to bottom, trimming knife, heavy craft knife and standard craft knife, used for all categories of modelmaking.*

Below *Clamps always come in useful. The toomakers clamps, at the top, are expensive but invaluable for advanced projects. The lower G-clamp is ideal for baseboard construction.*

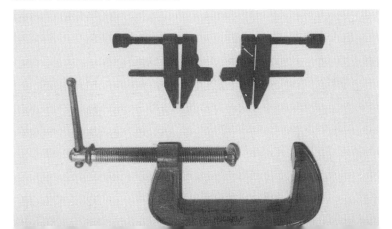

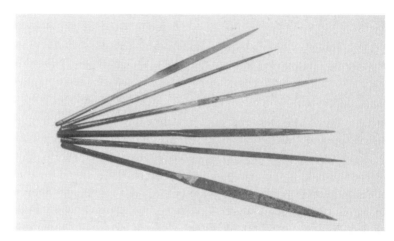

Needle files are required for fine modelmaking. They can be bought as sets or individually, and whilst fairly costly are invaluable.

the limit of available storage space. Their uses in any practical hobby are legion and as they cost nothing, it's pure folly not to use them.

To this list, I would add the highly convenient sets of plastic drawers that can be obtained from Woolworths and most hardware stores. Although they do have to be bought, they make the best possible use of space and this is often in even shorter supply than cash!

Needless to say, containers need to be labelled. Self-adhesive labels are reasonably cheap, and quite durable. The Dymo type labeller is more expensive but is neater and the resulting label is much more durable, particularly in workshop use where it gets touched with dirty hands.

Having collected the necessary materials, they need to be cut and formed into the required shape, then assembled in the correct order. To do this, one needs a toolkit. Although a great deal can be done, 'with a few simple tools' — to use a very common catchphrase — the idea that one can get along happily with very little is a fallacy. The correct tool not only speeds the work, it improves the quality of the end product. Furthermore, basic tools are one area where it is definitely false economy to cut costs. Fifty years ago I spent as much as a schoolboy could afford on a fretsaw. A couple of years ago I took a good hard look at it with a view to buying a new one, but decided in the end that its only fault was that, over the years, the two clamping bolts had got a trifle worn: two new bolts and wingnuts (well, two second-hand bolts and wingnuts out of the stock drawers) were all that was needed to give it a fresh lease of life. It will outlast me, as will the rest of my toolkit!

It is easy to say, with absolute truth, that the larger the toolkit, the easier it is to cut costs. For example, I have a Unimat SL lathe with most accessories, including the saw-table. With this I can not only turn loco fittings, I can produce stripwood of whatever size I want. On the face of it, two highly desirable features, and apparently very economical in practice. The lathe cost £200 several years ago, and that was a bargain price. You can buy a lot of loco fittings and stripwood for £200, but you'd be hard put to fit up my outfit today for twice that!

Your requirements will depend very much on what you are doing, but it is safe to say that the following tools will always be required:

6 in pin-ended miniature hacksaw
6 in flat second-cut file
6 in half round second-cut file
6 in three square (triangular) second-cut file
Small hammer, preferably cross pein
Centre punch
Engineer's square, 3 in to 4 in long
Drill brace
Selection of small twist drills
Large screwdriver
Small screwdriver
Large flat-nose pliers
Medium snipe nose pliers
Small flat nose pliers
Two wood chisels, $\frac{1}{4}$ in and $\frac{1}{2}$ in
Electric soldering iron
Craft-knife or scalpel
Heavy-duty trimming knife
Selection of sandpaper
Various adhesives
Small but firm vice and workbench

This list is by no means exhaustive, but with this small selection, most major modelling tasks can be performed.

Tools are an excellent investment, and some portion of the budget should be set aside for their acquisition. Most are

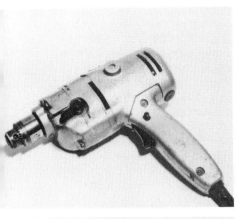

Left *The ubiquitous mains electric drill–so useful for household tasks that its cost should be set against the home budget.*

Below left *The power jigsaw, whilst not essential, saves an enormous amount of time and effort as well as making curved cuts as simple as straight ones. Again, invaluable around the home.*

Right *The 'Workmate'. This is not only the most versatile workbench so far produced, it is extremely portable and makes an excellent working platform for home decorating, etc. The jaws grip anything at any angle, and all in all, it is an essential tool for maintenance, its value for the hobby is merely a bonus.*

reasonable in price, but there are some fairly expensive items that are worth considering seriously. Two of these are invaluable, a mains-powered electric drill and a mains-powered jig-saw. Both are equally useful for household projects, and therefore I think that their cost can be justified on all grounds — but don't blame me if you end up rebuilding the kitchen before you are allowed to get on with the layout. I don't advise the jig-saw attachment for the drill, as you frequently need to use both tools at once, and the extra cost of the self-powered saw is worthwhile.

I don't recommend a power circular saw, even though I have one and find that in the sawbench it is extremely useful. Unfortunately, I can't say it is cost effective as most of the work can be done with a power jigsaw with very little extra bother.

The well-known Black & Decker 'Workmate' is an excellent portable workbench. It is also a useful working platform, and a lot of other things besides. It is the only modern innovative tool which has had universal acclaim from both the professional craftsman and the knowledgeable amateur. It is a good investment, but, once again is so useful for jobs around the house that it should not be set against the modelling budget.

A very useful addition to the modeller's toolkit is a miniature 12 v electric drill. These tools are reasonable in price and not only make the business of drilling small holes much easier, but can take a small arbor which carries a tiny abrasive disc. This will cut through rail — and almost anything else if given the chance — and solves a lot of tricky problems as the layout develops. The drill will also take discarded dentist's drills, which are rather useful for removing odd

bits of material in more advanced modelling projects.

There is one tool, fairly costly, which is a sound long term investment — the airbrush. Here it is advisable to ignore the low-price 'modeller's airbrushes', for although they are useful, they lack the precision of the proper tool, and are generally superseded very rapidly. Above all, avoid the aerosol propellants like the plague. I've an open mind on what they may do to the ozone layer, I'm more concerned by what they do to the budget — one expensive can goes nowhere! If you can't afford a compressor, use the car's spare tyre by means of an adaptor valve, with or without a footpump. You can keep the tyre very fully inflated on regular visits to the filling station.

One invaluable source of tools and low-cost raw materials is the model railway and model engineering exhibition. Over the years I have collected a quantity of useful material, metal and plastic, not to mention a large collection of screws, well below list prices, at such shows. In addition, most of the recent additions to my toolkit have also been purchased at shows.

The Model Engineer Exhibition, which is held annually in January at the Wembley Conference Centre, is an excellent place for the bargain hunter in search of material. It is also a good place to track down specialized tools. Other shows have their bargains — not only in materials, but in models as well, whilst the International Model Railway Exhibition, organized by the Model Railway Club each Easter is also a useful source of supplies.

In this connection, I'd draw your attention to an excellent firm that appears at both shows, Shesto, who offer, at keen prices, a wide range of top-quality tools, together with a lot of useful advice. This is a long-established concern, with modern ideas and old traditions, and whatever they sell is a good, quality tool.

Once upon a time there were numerous small shops which sold ex-government surplus goods. Most have gone, but Proops, of Tottenham Court Road remain. They are regular exhibitors at the Model Engineer Exhibition, and their stand is always stocked with interesting items. As well as carrying a wonderful selection of odds and ends, they have lately branched out into special ranges of inexpensive tools and electric switches. Their £1 bargain packs are well known and whilst some are more a lucky dip than anything else, the packs of screws, springs, washers and similar items are excellent value and justly famed. Their dishevelled emporium generally has a couple of bins of cheap, but completely reliable microswitches, and, not infrequently, one can obtain the famous

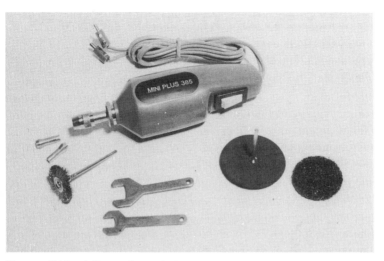

The small 12 v drill, together with the useful abrasive discs and a small wire brush. This tool saves its cost many times over with the reduction of breakage of small twist drills.

GPO 3000 relays at a very reasonable cost.

One reason Proops are still in business is that they play fair by their customers — goods are sold 'as seen', but the staff will usually given an honest and accurate opinion of the actual condition. In fact, a lot of their stock is unused and in excellent order. The main risk you run in entering their Aladdin's Cave is being tempted into buying some perfectly sound items that looked too good and cheap to resist, but for which you have absolutely no use whatsoever.

I will, therefore, end by pointing out that not all 'bargains' are necessarily useful, and therefore it is essential to go through your collection from time to time in order to weed out all that you come to realize is no use whatsoever. You can throw it away, but if it has a marginal value, and you're a member of a model railway club that holds an annual exhibition, you can always package it neatly and hope to sell it on the club bargain stand.

THE SITE FOR THE LAYOUT

Many railway modellers start out with the laudable idea of building the layout to end all layouts. As a long term objective, nothing could be better, but the simple fact is that this usually needs more space than is available initially. In my opinion, everyone should face up to the fact that he may well build several layouts in the course of his career. A small trial effort to test techniques makes excellent sense at the outset.

Even a small model railway is quite a large item by most standards, and as a result, some sort of home is essential. Despite the potential of the portable layout, which I will discuss in the next chapter, there is no doubt that a permanent railway room is far and away the most convenient with, as a second choice, a site where the railway can remain permanently erected without affecting the other uses of the room. As the model is going to be of a considerable size, one does need a fairly generous area to devote to the layout and this can create quite a few problems. The average house has a large number of locations where some sort of model can be fitted in and my booklet *A Home For Your Railway* (Peco) shows most of them. I propose to look in some detail here at the more promising locations.

The garage is a sound, weatherproof structure that is built to a simple specification, and measures not less than approximately 5 m x 2.5 m. By one of those fortunate co-incidences, this happens to be a very useful sized room for a model railway, large enough for an interesting layout of almost any description or scale, yet not so enormous as to cost the proverbial arm and a leg to develop.

There are several possibilities. One is to construct a narrow shelf layout around the walls, high enough to clear the car. This is probably the best arrangement where the budget is tight since a sizeable, if relatively simple layout can be built within this specification, as shown in Figs 3/1 and 3/2. Clearly, with such an arrangement, a small car is more convenient, but I've found that one can happily get a reasonable layout around a Ford Escort, so the car needn't be too small.

The second possibility, only practical on older houses where the garage lies behind the house and is approached by a side passage, is to erect a carport (Fig 3/3). This then releases the garage for better use. Of course, there is no need to have a carport. Judging by my neighbours, I am not alone in feeling that there are better things to do with a garage than keep a car in it. There is, indeed, a body of

Right Fig 3/1 *Cross section of a typical garage showing arrangement of layout.*

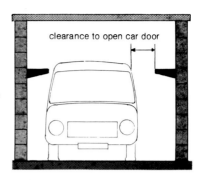

clearance to open car door

Below Fig 32 *Plan of typical garage layout allowing for housing of car.*

Bottom Fig 3/3 *Erecting a carport to free garage for layout.*

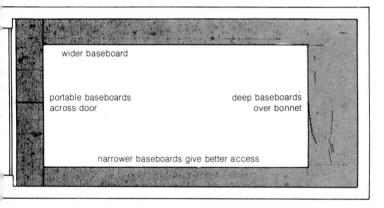

wider baseboard

portable baseboards across door

deep baseboards over bonnet

narrower baseboards give better access

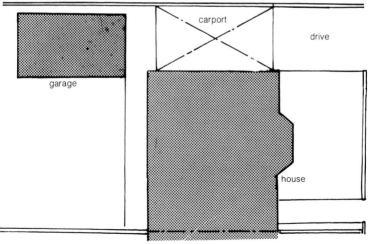

carport

drive

garage

house

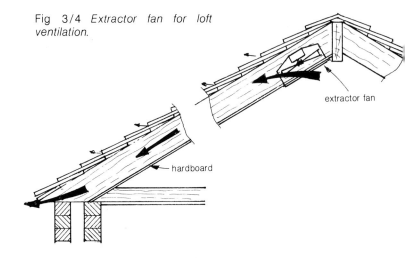

Fig 3/4 *Extractor fan for loft ventilation.*

extractor fan

hardboard

opinion which suggests that it is a bad thing to put a wet car in a garage, though I do have a suspicion that the fellow who first put the idea forward was a railway modeller!

The loft is a traditional location, and, providing the job is done correctly, has much to commend it. The overall cost is likely to be appreciable, but on a DIY basis, almost certainly using second-hand timber, it can be spread over a period of time. Properly organized, the loft will also provide storage for a host of useable, but temporarily unwanted household goods. It has two snags, the noise can annoy the rest of the household, and dust and dirt from the construction of the layout does fall into the home. A spare vacuum cleaner, preferably of the cylinder pattern, permanently located in the loft area is, I feel, very desirable.

Most lofts have poor ventilation, and it is essential to attend to this. A very simple answer is an extractor fan blowing stale and hot air down an improvized trunking formed by blocking in the space between two rafters. This is shown in Fig 3/4. This extremely simple dodge works well, creating a steady flow of air which cools the loft space even in high summer. Good insulation — which helps improve the heating of the house, takes care of winter chills, and one can end up with a sizeable railway room which access in the centre of the layout.

Spare bedrooms are *not* a good idea, Murphy's Law states categorically, that as soon as any layout built in a spare bedroom

24

has reached a reasonable state of completion, the spare bedroom is required as a spare bedroom. On the other hand, there was once a cartoon in the *Model Railroader*, I think, showing a wife consoling her husband after a family wedding with the following words, 'Don't think of it as losing a daughter, think of it as gaining a room for your railroad'.

One handy site is the large cupboard or small boxroom, such as can occasionally be found in an older house. In my opinion, a permanent site 2 m x 1.5 m is ideal for a compact economical starter layout in 4 mm scale or less. Whilst one is rather limited in scope, the model can be worked up to a very high standard indeed without either involving you in an enormous amount of work or stretching a small budget too far. I once constructed a layout in the cupboard under the stairs on the lines of Fig 3/5. It had its faults, but these had

Right *This photo shows a corner of Frank Colson's small GWR branch layout that was housed in a large cupboard in an old terraced house in Bristol. It is an early post-war model, still using the obsolete outside third pickup, and by current standards, not fully 'scenified'.*

Below Fig 3/5 *Layout in under-stair cupboard. The fiddle yard hinges sideways to clear the passage.*

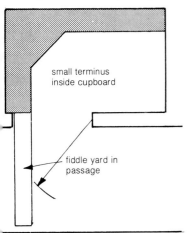

small terminus
inside cupboard

fiddle yard in
passage

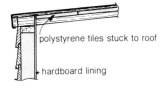

polystyrene tiles stuck to roof

hardboard lining

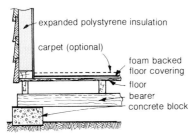

expanded polystyrene insulation

carpet (optional)

foam backed
floor covering

floor

bearer

concrete block

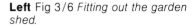

Left Fig 3/6 *Fitting out the garden shed.*

Right *A small garden shed which can house a compact, economical layout and a useful workshop as well.*

nothing to do with the site or the basic design, and I'd thoroughly recommend this option.

The wooden garden shed makes an excellent and reasonably economical site, providing you realize that it will cost as much again to fit it out properly as it will to buy it in the first place. In particular, you need to be able to provide a proper electricity supply, and to do so in accordance with the IEE regulations is not cheap — though it is both safe and convenient. I don't propose to go further, since if you don't know the regulations you must employ a qualified electrician. Electricity at 240v 50Hz is potentially lethal, nowhere more so than out of doors, where one may be standing on damp earth.

It is also advisable to insulate the shed thermally. This is not necessarily a costly business, since the walls can be lined with hardboard, or if you feel the budget can be stretched slightly, with plastic-coated ply wallboard, which not only looks very good indeed, but needs no further decorative treatment other than an occasional wipe down with a damp cloth. The void between the lining and the outer wall forms an insulation gap of sorts, but it is better to fill it with insulation provided by polystyrene foam packing, large quantities of which are thrown away by your local high street stores every week. The base should be raised on blocks and protected against damp, and the floor covered with a good foam-based floor covering — a remnant from your local furnishing company is ideal as the colour and pattern is irrelevant. You can further increase the insulation by laying a carpet on the floor, whilst

a 750 watt high-level heater is quite adequate and extremely safe. Fig 3/6 shows the general arrangement.

Having mentioned heating, I would point out that there is no need to keep a railway room as warm as a normal living room. Indeed, in my youth, one rarely bothered to heat them at all, and one was advised that clockwork O gauge layouts should not be used in midwinter since, when temperatures fell below 35° (Farenheit, of course), the springs became brittle. Whilst I feel that one should not let temperatures fall below 5° (Celsius, of course), something between this and 10° is quite tolerable providing there are no draughts, and that you wear warm clothing, in particular, good socks and footwear. However, given a reasonable level of tungsten lighting — which in my opinion, should be bright enough to permit good photography without additional lighting — the average railway room will get very snug very quickly.

The garden shed brings us logically to thoughts of a home extension. The principle of home extension, or for that matter, moving up market to a larger house, is firmly established, and there are many straightforward schemes available to allow one to finance this out of income, but excellent though these may be it still costs money.

This brings us straight to the question of the size of the budget. It is very easy, particularly if you happen to be listening to the home extension salesman at the time, to overlook the point that the extra cost of the extension, whether it be through a loan or an increase in the mortgage, has to be found out of the same income that must, not

Alan Wright's 'Cheviotdale' fitted into a small outhouse. Trains were short, curves tight, but with careful selection of stock, no problems arose. Being built on sectional baseboards, it could be taken to exhibitions, or stored whilst other layouts were erected in the same space.

only pay the mortgage, but feed and clothe the family, provide, through insurance, for possible mishaps and disasters, run the family car, pay for holidays and entertainment, meet rates, taxes and similar impositions and, hopefully, have a little left over for hobbies. If you miscalculate, you know what must lose out — the model railway. There are few things worse than buying a beautiful railway room and then discovering that you can't afford the railway to put in it!

So, I seriously advise that any question of adding a special railway room should be left until you have amassed enough material, locomotives, coaches, wagons, track, points, power units, the odd kilometre or so of layout wire, a large stock of timber and ply, plus a load of other raw material so that you can proceed to build the railway of your dreams without having to dig too deeply into your pocket. Furthermore, an excellent way of financing the extension is through a short term endowment insurance taken out some years in advance, rather than through borrowing, for all that a home loan currently attracts tax relief on the interest. Meantime a small portable layout, or a tiny wall-hugging system fitted into one of the existing rooms of the house is the best starting point.

THE PORTABLE LAYOUT

When the budget is limited, a separate railway room is almost certainly an unimaginable luxury. By all means make long term plans for what is, without a doubt, the ideal arrangement, but in the meantime, exploit what you have available. There are many ways of squeezing a small layout into odd corners of the home, but on the whole, the most convenient solution to this particular problem is the portable layout. However, a lot of newcomers fall into a very common trap and completely fail to realize the overall requirements of portability, with the result that the scheme becomes completely unwieldy. I shall be dealing with suitable track plans in a later chapter, and covering constructional details elsewhere, in this chapter I intend to deal solely with the essential requirements of a truly portable system.

The initial error is all too easy to make, that a portable layout ought to be a single unit. This is just about possible in N gauge, where a worthwhile scheme can be built up on a flush door panel. In OO and HO even a baseboard as large and unweildy as 1.8 m by 1.2 m is far too small for anything but a toy-like scheme. Many years ago, Peter Denny, who built one of the earliest high-quality portable layouts to be shown in public, suggested that if the individual unit was appreciably larger than 1.2 m by 0.6 m, it would be extremely inconvenient. This is not an absolute requirement, but any appreciable excess above these dimensions needs to be very carefully considered since it is difficult to get anything larger through a normal doorway, or along a narrow passageway, particularly if you are doing it on your own — as is usually the case.

You will find exhibition layouts with considerably larger baseboard sections, but they are used under conditions radically different from those experienced by the home system. For a start, they are built by clubs and are moved around by a small, well-trained team. Furthermore, club-rooms generally have easier access than a home, whilst any hall suitable for public exhibitions must, by law, have wide entrances. Last, and perhaps most important of all, they are not portable layouts to begin with, they are either erected for long periods, or simply stored between shows.

Although a portable layout is one which is built in sections for ease of removal, not all layouts built in sections are portable. Where the layout is normally erected in a permanent site, but is, on occasions moved (such as to exhibitions) it is a transportable layout. Such a model is only moved on rare occasions and so it is

Above left *Erecting the second 'Buckingham' in its home in a London flat. To the extreme left, the main section has already been erected, the corner section is going in place, and Peter is locating the only legs on this section.*

Left *Fitting a short filler section into the second 'Buckingham'. This was used to link to the shortened version of the layout—one of the advantages of a well-designed portable layout.*

Above *The second 'Buckingham', in its shortened version, fully erected in a modest-sized living room. Note the fully braced legs on the initial section on the left, with simpler versions on the rest.*

possible to accept not only the occasional inconvenience but, in addition, the fact that dismantling and re-erection may take all of ten hours.

The home layout has to be moved and erected by one individual. There are exceptions, where a father-son team are on hand for instance, but even here, sons have been known to leave home eventually. Wives are rarely sufficiently motivated to help with heavy lifting, this is the best way to turn a layout into 'That thing of yours'.

In addition, the home layout needs to be easy to assemble. It must

Above Nick Freezer's 'Dugdale Road' in its original fully portable form, more or less ready for transit. The fiddle yard is on the top of the four-fold system. Screw-in legs provide a simple and rigid form of support.

Left Screwing legs into the upper section of 'Dugdale Road'. Whilst home-made legs are cheaper, this arrangement is probably the most economical approach where simplicity is required. The screw-in plates are useful baseboard braces at the vulnerable corners.

Right 'Dugdale Road' erected. This photograph shows it in extended form, with an additional section included to give a longer platform.

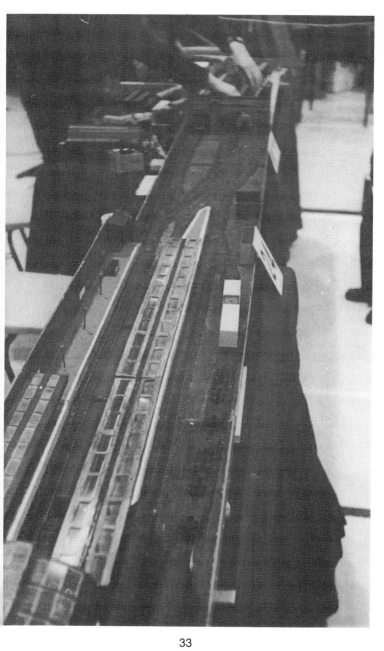

be possible to take it from storage, erect it, put the stock on the tracks, enjoy a worthwhile operating session, then remove the stock, store it safely, dismantle the layout and put it away within the course of a single evening — and still get to bed by midnight! This puts a top limit on the size of the portable layout. Any unit of a portable layout must be of a size and shape that its builder and owner can easily pick up and carry it through the house without doing any damage en route. I'm not quite sure which is the more serious, wrecking part of the model or scratching a wall but I'm convinced neither is exactly desirable. As for breaking an ornament — need I point out that, no matter how hideous it might be, it turns, in fragments, into an object of great sentimental value?

During the process of assembly, it is often necessary to support the baseboard with one hand whilst adjusting the legs with the other, the question of weight does become quite important. Another consideration that affects the overall size is the normal storage place. My eldest son's 'Dugdale Road' had its initial dimensions fixed by the capacity of a small cupboard in his room at University Hall, 750 mm by 280 mm. Where a suitable cupboard, or alcove exists, then the layout units should be made to fit.

Consideration should also be given to the family car which is usually the most convenient way to get the layout to an exhibition hall, or any other venue, such as a church fete or school fund-raising drive. It is therefore, a good idea to make the sections of a size and shape to fit comfortably into the back. I will go so far as to suggest that if the layout can't be packed into your car, it isn't really portable.

These considerations suggest to me that a layout based on a 1 m by 0.5 m unit is a reasonable proposition, particularly as two or three such units give ample room for an 00 gauge station — underscale, of course, but an agreeable compromise. There is no need to make all sections identical, although it is advisable to make the larger units as mirror image pairs. In this way they can be stored face to face, with a spacer come protective section bolted each end as in Fig 4/1. Alternatively, where the baseboards have an integral backscene, the backscenes can be employed for this purpose, as in Fig 4/2. It is worth remembering that although this saves a lot of material, the very delicate track ends are particularly vulnerable and really need the sort of physical protection which is provided by the end spacers.

One popular arrangement is to make the units fold in the centre but where this is done it is essential to watch weight, as a heavy unit

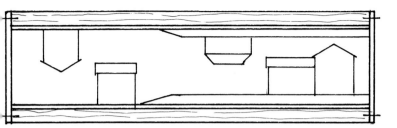

Fig 4/1 *Pairs of baseboards face to face and separated by end spacers.*

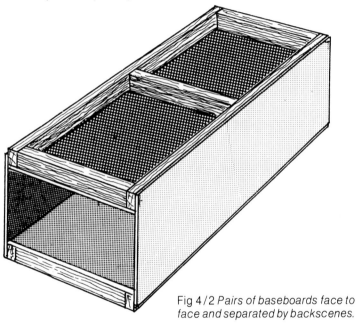

Fig 4/2 *Pairs of baseboards face to face and separated by backscenes.*

is particularly cumbersome, no matter what its dimensions might be. The basic principles are shown in Fig 4/3, whilst Fig 4/4 shows a multi-fold layout incorporating a turntable pattern fiddle yard, suitable designs for these boards will appear in a later chapter.

One virtue of the sectional layout is that you need only work on one two or, at the most, three units at a time. As each sections takes some time to develop, you are not involved in an enormous outlay on any one occasion. Furthermore, with a sectional layout it is

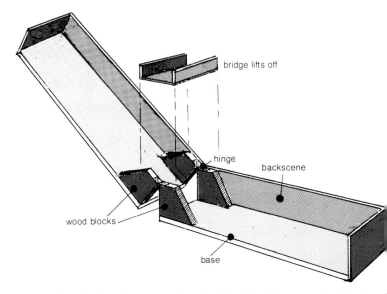

bridge lifts off

hinge

backscene

wood blocks

base

Above Fig 4/3 *Folding layout, showing how the hinge may be disguised with a bridge. A suitable layout plan appears in the following chapter.*

Below Fig 4/4 *Multi-fold scheme for portable layout. The inset sketch shows how the sections fold up. A suitable layout plan appears in the following chapter.*

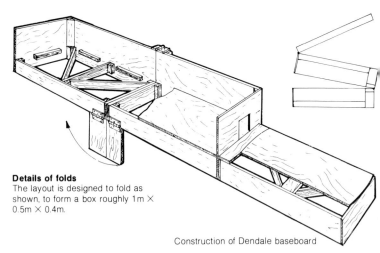

Details of folds
The layout is designed to fold as shown, to form a box roughly 1m × 0.5m × 0.4m.

Construction of Dendale baseboard

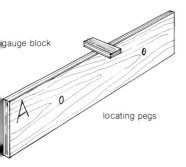

gauge block

locating pegs

A

Left Fig 4/5 *Jig for ensuring uni-formity at baseboard joints.*

Below Fig 4/6 *Using a hinge to connect baseboard sections.*

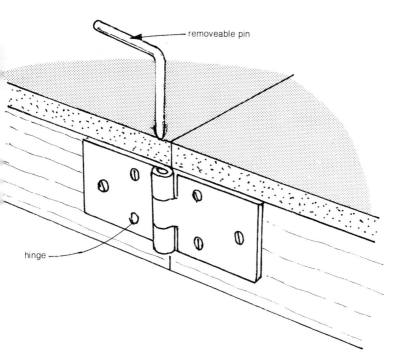

removeable pin

hinge

elatively easy to arrange for extension.

Indeed, it is feasible to devise a standardized baseboard nterface, so that the layout can be assembled in a variety of ways. his idea can be overdone, the American 'Modular' system is a case in point, where virtually everything is standardized. This is not s flexible as a standard interface for double or single track, which

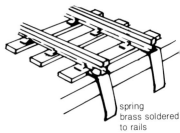

spring
brass soldered
to rails

Left *A baseboard joint made with a 'broken hinge' connector, as described in the text.*

Above Fig 4/7 *Electrical contacts across baseboard joints.*

allows one to design any sort of station or main line unit, probably on two or three conveniently sized baseboards, which do not have to be to any predetermined size or shape and which can be linked to any other unit at will. Where such an arrangement is contemplated it is advisable to construct a jig (Fig 4/5), to ensure that baseboard connections and tracks are always correctly aligned. Don't rely on measurement alone for this vital feature.

Baseboard sections can be held together in a variety of ways. One is to bolt them together with coach bolts and wing-nuts. This is a fairly slow method and so there is a lot to be said for the 'broken hinge' joint which is shown in Fig 4/6. Any commercial hinge is a fairly precise device — it must be if it is to work at all. It is comparatively cheap, especially if you can track down an old fashioned ironmonger who sells hinges out of boxes, rather than dispenses them on attractive bubblepacks at a 50 per cent increase in cost. You need the simple flap hinge, something between 2.5 cm and 5 cm in depth.

Remove the hinge pin by filing off one end and then, with a thin punch (a nail with the point filed off will do nicely), push out the old pin. It is then replaced with a close fitting wire pin, once again, a round nail will do the trick, and the hinge is then screwed across the joint. To separate the two sections, pull out the pins on either side and put them safely away in a small, labelled box. Don't leave them in the hinges, they'll only fall out as you move the sections around and you'll never find them again.

You don't hope that the tracks stay in line on their own, it essential to secure them firmly in place. My favourite system with flexible track is to insert small countersunk woodscrews into the framing on either side of the rails and to solder the rails to the screwheads. With soldered track, either the track pins are driven into the baseboard, or the end PCB sleepers are firmly fixed to the framing, giving the necessary rigidity of location.

Electrical connections across portable baseboards often cause some worry, but in practice there are two straightforward solutions. One solution makes use of a series of springy brass contacts across the baseboard joint. As Fig 4/7 shows, these can be soldered to the rail fixings, saving a great deal of trouble (though on many layouts, some additional contacts are needed for other circuits). This is a relatively cheap and very reliable method, providing the layout is not left erected for considerable lengths of time. Dirt has a nasty habit of getting between the contact blades and although it is not too difficult to cure — a nail file pushed down the gap works wonders — this sort of intermittent fault is extremely annoying. Incidentally, don't use baseboard joints as section gaps, or Murphy's law arranges for the parts to touch and produce the most mysterious short circuits that defy location.

Multi-pin plugs and sockets provide a positive connection, the 'D' type plugs and sockets used primarily on computers and other electronic devices are excellent for the purpose, but they're not exactly cheap and you need a fair number. Ex-equipment plugs and sockets do come on the market from time to time at not-unreasonable prices. There are other sources one can exploit, I was delighted to find, in a worn-out colour TV, a whole mass of these useful gadgets which have been carefully put aside for future use. As an alternative, jumper cables using the relatively inexpensive audio plugs which are available in most high street electronic stores can be considered.

If multi-pin plugs are employed, it will generally be found best to construct a separate control panel from which individual umbilical leads snake out to the various sections, as shown in Fig 4/8. With this approach, it is a positive benefit if the plugs and sockets are a completely heterogeneous bunch, acquired as and when you can. The easiest way to avoid plugging the wrong plug in the right socket is to ensure that every socket is totally different!

Legs are probably the main problem with portable layouts, for they need to be firm and well-braced. As a result, it is a good idea to keep the layout reasonably low, certainly not more than about 1 m high, preferably something lower. Hinged legs, as shown in Fig 4/9,

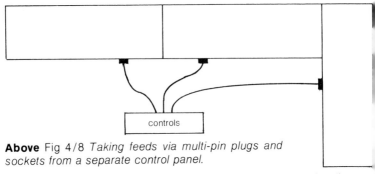

Above Fig 4/8 *Taking feeds via multi-pin plugs and sockets from a separate control panel.*

Below Fig 4/9 *Folding legs for portable baseboards. Note the diagonal struts to hold legs secure and that only the initial baseboard requires two pairs of legs.*

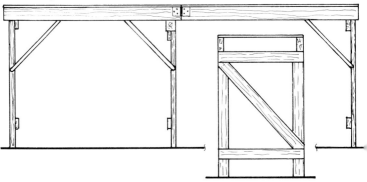

are the favourite arrangement. Only the initial baseboard section actually needs legs at each end, as the subsequent sections are supported at one end by the initial section.

Whenever there is a possibility of removal, a portable layout appears to make good sense, but it would be a mistake to suggest that it is, automatically, going to fit into the new home. This is rarely the case where the model has been tailor made to fit into a specific site, since the new house is highly unlikely to be identical in floor plan. One friend, then a serving officer in the RAF, a profession where removal is an occupational hazard, thought he has the answer for RAF married quarters are built to near identical designs. It worked like a dream, until he received a well-deserved promotion and qualified for a larger house! Well, the layout certainly went into the new spare bedroom, but it was by no means easy for anything or anyone else to get into the room when it was erected!

ECONOMICAL TRACK PLANS

A simple, yet satisfying layout design is probably the best approach to the hobby. It is certainly a very economical one, and here I would like to consider just a few straightforward schemes that come under the heading 'tried and tested'. It's as well, at this point to stress that absolute originality is impossible within the confines of a simple layout, every workable theme has been built at least a dozen times over. Come to think of it, quite a few unworkable ideas have been tried out as well. This doesn't mean that the resulting layout need resemble any of the others built to more or less the same basic plan. It's surprising how a few simple changes to the details — station buildings, goods shed, scenery etc, can completely transform the appearance of the model. The schemes are all drawn for 4 mm scale, but may be adapted to any of the other popular sizes, with suitable adjustments to baseboard lengths.

The first scheme, shown in Fig 5/1, is A. R. Walkley's classic 'Railway in a Suitcase' of 1926. A later, better-known version, Alan Wright's 'Inglenook Sidings', which differed only in general scenic treatment and the absence of the loco shed has been seen at many exhibitions, though it is now retired from the circuit.

This basic scheme, which requires just one shunting locomotive, steam diesel or even electric, plus around eight wagons, all fitted with auto-couplers, is about the cheapest start one can make in the serious side of the hobby. Whilst you can't enjoy the spectacle of trains going round and round and round and round again on a small oval, you've probably had your fill of this on your original train set. Operation can be even more interesting if you use Alan Wright's 'tiddlewink computer' to select four wagons at random which have to be shunted into a specific order. The idea is to have a selection of counters, each marked to correspond with one wagon, and to select

Fig 5/1 Walkley's original 'Railway in a Suitcase' of 1926—still a sound scheme for the present day.

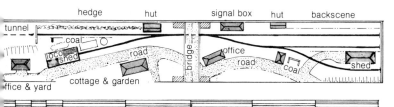

Alan Wright's 'Inglenook Sidings', a simple shunting layout following the principle of A.R. Walkley's 'Railway in a Suitcase' of 1926.

four at random and then assemble the train in the order of drawing. This particular requirement has defeated a professional railwayman who, used to a much longer shunting neck, didn't realize that so many moves would be needed to get the wagons into order. At all events, it will provide a lot of fun from the outset and can be built into something larger without too much difficulty.

The branch line model, built on portable modules, with a terminus feeding a fiddle yard, is, for steam age modellers, an excellent economical start. Indeed, when it was first proposed, the idea was to build a small branch terminus that could, later, be incorporated into a larger main line system, but the branch line theme proved so popular that this particular aspect became overlooked. It's worth keeping in mind.

Obviously, the fact that a high degree of realism is possible with so little allows one to build a small branch line on a fairly tight budget. So in Fig 5/2 I show a basic branch terminus which is a close copy of Peter Denny's 'Stony Stratford', and is about the simplest arrangement one can have for a small terminus. Although it is probably too simple to retain interest for very long, it makes an ideal test bed to see how you get on with some of the modelling techniques I describe in this book.

A slightly larger scheme, Fig 5/3, is designed to fit onto three

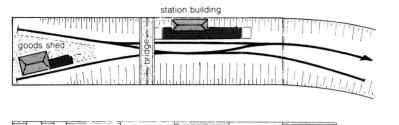

Fig 5/2 *A minimum-sized branch terminus based on Peter Denny's 'Stony Stratford'.*

folding boards — the construction of which was shown in Chapter 4. It's still a fairly simple layout, just about as small as one can get and retain interest. There is a short bay, which I would suggest be used mainly for parcel and milk vans, a siding leading to a cattle dock and two general sidings to the front of the layout. The terminus serves a small market town which would be represented on the backscene, the only non-railway building shown is a pub, which always makes an interesting model and was often found close to the railway.

To the extreme left we have a simple turntable fiddle yard. For those unused to the concept, the principle is simple, the trains run 'offstage' into a set of storage roads where they are re-marshalled and returned. As it is customary to re-arrange trains by lifting the stock off the track, the name is self-explanatory. The fiddle yard represents the rest of the railway system, it saves in space and cost, and provides a lot of storage for trains. In this case the fiddle yard can be turned end for end as a turntable. This is workable because trains are relatively short, but where larger trains are wanted, the

Fig 5/3 *'Dendale', a slightly more elaborate branch terminus built on a three-fold portable baseboard.*

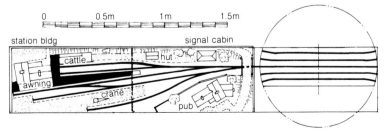

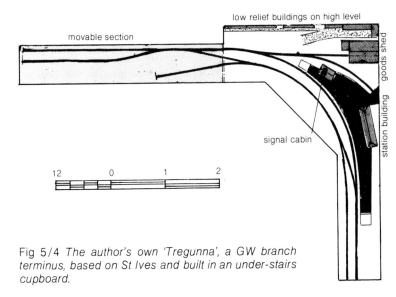

low relief buildings on high level

movable section

goods shed

station building

signal cabin

12   0   1   2

Fig 5/4 *The author's own 'Tregunna', a GW branch terminus, based on St Ives and built in an under-stairs cupboard.*

sector plate is preferable. Although there are many ways of arranging the multiple storage roads in a fiddle yard, where economy is the watchword, the sector plate or turntable is cheapest — there are no turnouts to buy or build — and providing the sector plate or turntable is moved by hand it is an extremely satisfactory solution.

Still keeping to the ultra-small theme, Fig 5/4 shows my own 'Tregunna', which I built in the cupboard under the stairs in our first

Fig 5/5 *'Shillingford', a straightforward terminus capable of simple extension.*

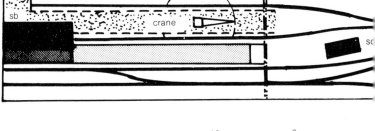

sb

crane

sc

Shillingbury

12   0

married home. It is based on St Ives in Cornwall, and was great fun. Whilst I'd never consider building it again — I've a feeling a lot of the pleasure I got came out of the time in my life when I built it, it's certainly a design I'd heartily recommend to a newcomer.

The branch line terminus scheme in Fig 5/5 shows how a design may be made extendable, for the third baseboard — loco shed can be constructed some time after the first part has been completed. As usual, the line ends in a fiddle yard.

If this sort of thing isn't to your taste, as you want to run main line trains, either steam or diesel, Fig 5/6 is a development of my popular 'Minories' main line terminus layout, also arranged in modular fashion for steady expansion, adding junction, goods yard, loco shed and anything else that might occur to you as and when you feel ready to tackle the model. In this instance, it is also possible to lengthen the station platforms by the insertion of a simple baseboard section. This happens to be a very convenient arrangement, indeed, my son's 'Dugdale Road' has had its trackage extended by some 300 per cent in this fashion without the addition of a single extra turnout.

These schemes are designed for sectional baseboards, but if a permanent site is available, something more is possible. In Fig 5/7 I show a simple scheme which fits into a small garden shed and is based on a layout I built some years ago. The plan differs from the original in the addition of a halt on the main line, the original was constructed in my workshop and was more a test track than a working layout. I've extended the scenic development with the idea of giving more interest as a layout. It has one snag — the operation is very limited. Indeed, you can only consider three trains at once and one of these is very short, a railcar or single coach push-pull which is normally stabled in the bay road in the main station.

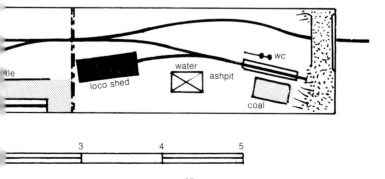

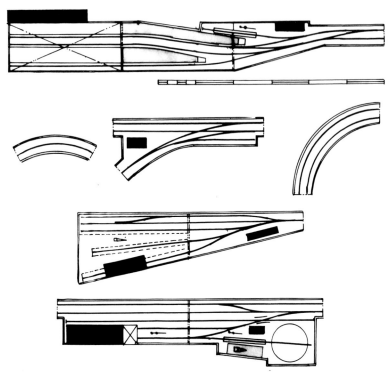

Fig 5/6 *'Minories', something of a minor classic, a compact main line terminus, with extensions that can be built as resources permit.*

The suggested rolling stock, for a GW branch, is given below:

Train 1: '43XX' 'Mogul' + two coaches: B set or two clerestory corridor.
Train 2: '57XX' 0-6-WPT + five wagons and brake van.
Train 3: '48XX'/'14XX' 0-4-2T + auto-trailer or diesel railcar.
Additional stock — four to six wagons or vans.

Needless to say, you can have additional items but this is all you can put on the track at any one time, if you want to be able to move anything! Only one train can run at any one time, the other three have to be in a siding or in the loop.

In Fig 5/8 we have a more elaborate scheme, a standard 'L'-shaped terminus fiddle yard scheme to fit permanently into the

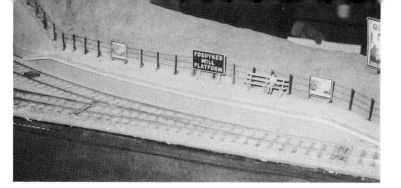

Above *A halt is the basic station, just a platform with possibly one siding for local freight. Whilst, on its own, lacking in operational interest—very little happens here—as a secondary station on a small layout it provides welcome variety and the opportunity for extra modelling.*

Below Fig 5/7 *A simple single-track layout fitted into a small garden shed.*

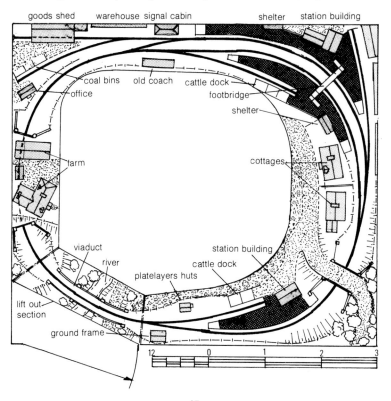

goods shed   warehouse signal cabin   shelter   station building

coal bins   old coach   cattle dock

office

footbridge

shelter

farm

cottages

viaduct

river

platelayers huts

station building

cattle dock

lift out
section

ground frame

12   0   1   2   3

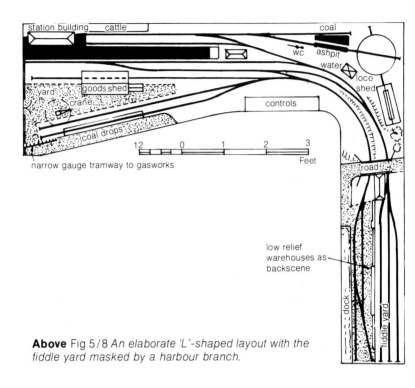

station building   cattle

coal

wc   ashpit

water

loco shed

yard   goods shed   crane

controls

coal drops

12   0   1   2   3

Feet

narrow gauge tramway to gasworks

road

low relief
warehouses as
backscene

dock

fiddle yard

Above Fig 5/8 *An elaborate 'L'-shaped layout with the fiddle yard masked by a harbour branch.*

Below Fig 5/9 *A main line terminus scheme designed to fit comfortably into a garage and still provide ample room for storing the car.*

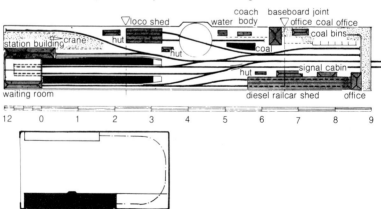

coach   baseboard joint

loco shed   water   body   office   coal office

coal bins

station building   crane   hut

hut   coal

signal cabin

hut

waiting room

diesel railcar shed   office

12   0   1   2   3   4   5   6   7   8   9

The sliding fiddle yard on Alan Wright's 'Cheviotdale'. The five storage roads each take the longest train the layout can handle, thus allowing for plenty of variety in the service.

corner of a room of reasonable size. The fiddle yard is hidden behind a model quayside, which adds to the operational interest of the layout. There is a fully fledged loco depot, complete with turntable just large enough to take a 4-4-0 and sufficient siding space for a reasonable amount of freight stock. The siding to the front is solely for coal, and has a small narrow gauge line which takes coal to the 'offstage' gasworks. It is easy, with North Sea gas, to forget that for over 100 years, town gas was produced in local gasworks from coal brought by railway, and that, in a steam age model, a gasworks adds to the operating pleasure.

The final design, Fig 5/9, is intended to fit into a standard garage and provide room for the car as well. The main station is located along one wall, and is built on sectional baseboards so that it, and the fiddle yard on the other side, may be taken down and carried to an exhibition (inside the family car, I should add!). The rest of the line would, I suggest, be permanently erected in the garage, ideally, bracketed off the walls. If clearances were tight, you could dismantle the terminus and store it at the far end, leaving ample room to drive in.

BASEBOARDS AT LOW COST

Baseboards are a necessary evil: they are absolutely essential, yet they can, all too easily consume a great deal of one's capital. Worse still, this expenditure comes at the very outset of layout construction so there is a temptation to skimp on material. I cannot over-emphasize the point that careless cost-cutting in this area leads to heartbreak for, if the baseboard begins to fail, the entire layout is useless and has to be scrapped.

Having said that, there are several ways of reducing the outlay on the framing. The most promising is that covered in earlier chapters, to design the layout on a modular basis, thus spreading the cost over a greater period of time. Equally worthwhile is the use of second-hand timber, or suitable offcuts bought cheaply. Providing it is free from dry or wet rot and active woodworm, second-hand timber has one undeniable virtue, it is well seasoned and unlikely to warp after it has been built into the model. Here, access to a sawbench can be invaluable as the more economical sizes are rarely ideal for our needs. For example, second-hand floorboards are reasonable cheap, but the wrong shape. Split into three equal widths, you have an ample supply of baseboard framing for the classic rectangular frame shown in Fig 6/1. This type of framing is simple and well tested, but not always economical.

One can, in certain circumstances, reduce the amount of timber involved by a simple change in design. An obvious way of reducing costs is to use smaller section timber, and although this needs to be approached carefully, lest the framing becomes too weak, it is a worthwhile approach where smaller sized modules are employed. Fig 6/2 depicts a suitable frame for a solid top baseboard not exceeding 1 m x 350 mm in size. Here the plywood surface forms an integral part of the construction, and is not an addition to a self-supporting frame. Although lighter — and cheaper — than the conventional framing, I know it is strong enough and rigid enough to withstand years of use. It is also considerably lighter, an important point where portability is concerned.

Plywood, when correctly used, provides a very strong lightweight framing. This has, in the past been overlooked through a failure to appreciate one simple structural design principle. The strength of a beam is more related to its depth than to its thickness, so, given a depth from 50 mm to 100 mm dependant on length, 6 mm thick ply makes an admirable framing for baseboards. The only other material required is square timber for the joints. The photographs

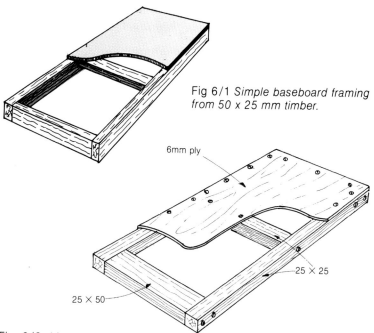

Fig 6/1 *Simple baseboard framing from 50 x 25 mm timber.*

6mm ply

25 × 25

25 × 50

Fig 6/2 *Lightweight framing for small baseboard.*

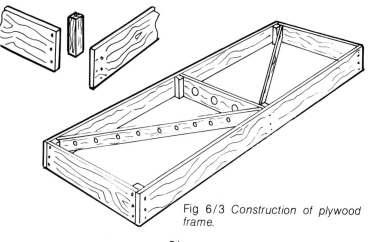

Fig 6/3 *Construction of plywood frame.*

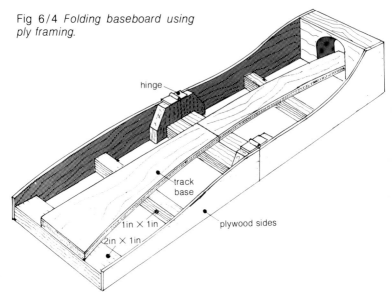

Fig 6/4 *Folding baseboard using ply framing.*

hinge

track base

plywood sides

1in × 1in

2in × 1in

show some baseboards I built several years ago, using 9 mm thick ply. Experience here revealed that, as one tends to do in early experiments, I'd overdone matters. Fig 6/3 shows the construction of this type of framing. The diagonal bracing is not absolutely essential, providing the joints are properly made, preferably by glueing and screwing.

In Fig 6/4 I show how a folding baseboard can be constructed from ply framing, using odd offcuts of timber. It is a modernized version of a system used by Peter Denny in the late 1940s, using lengths of timber from packing crates.

The construction of a ply framing is certainly eased with power saws, but the traditional handsaw is perfectly suitable. The main problem here is supporting a nominal '8 ft x 4 ft' sheet at a comfortable height for cutting. There are two alternatives available: one is to do a little pre-planning and get the timber merchant to saw the sheet into planks; the other is to support the sheet on the floor of the garage, or on some other suitable flat surface, by means of timber blocks or even house bricks, go down on your hands and knees and get to work with a sharp tenon saw. Again, a little pre-planning assists, as you can often reduce the panel into three or four more manageable sections which can then be handled on a suitable sawhorse. The Black & Decker 'Workmate' is extremely convenient for this, but in the past I've done a great deal of work with

Above *Baseboard with ply framing under construction. Note how much of the central cross bracing has been cut away for lightness.*

Below *Ply framing with top surface in place. Note the clamp used temporarily to hold baseboard sections together.*

Multi-level construction in ply. The road and river-bed was made up from smaller offcuts from the main sheet.

no more equipment than a kitchen stool and a couple of G-clamps

Of course, the outlay on a complete sheet of ply may be prohibitive, but, providing your baseboard module is kept fairly small, a lot can be done with smaller pieces. Old tea chests contain a large amount of quite good ply, and although they are no longer so readily obtainable as in my youth, you can see them advertised for around £1 each. The ply is thin, but two thickness of 3 mm are just as good as one piece of 6 mm, providing you stick them together with a reliable woodworking glue. With this form of composite construction, it is quite easy to use relatively short lengths to make a reasonable sized beam, providing the overlap is generous. Fig 6/5 shows the general idea. Don't screw the pieces together — glue and pin, holding the joints with G-clamps for at least twelve hours to allow the glue to harden. With composite construction, it pays to move slowly. If you can, leave your frames to harden for a week before moving on to the assembly stage.

Open-top construction is a very economical arrangement. In place of a single sheet of board covering the entire framework, bases are only provided where necessary to carry the tracks. Apar from the considerable saving on material, it also reduces the dead weight, and aids scenic development. In Fig 6/6 I show a fairly conventional approach. Although the track base is shown as a single piece of material, cut to shape, it is possible to construct bases out of any odd bit of suitable material to hand. It isn't even essential to have everything the same thickness, though you should, in general, aim at something between 9 mm and 12 mm. You can use filler strips to make up any difference between various parts

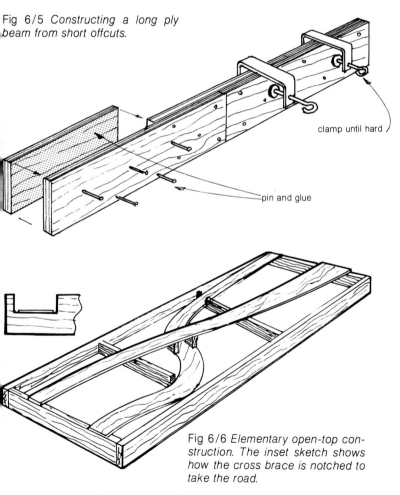

Fig 6/5 *Constructing a long ply beam from short offcuts.*

clamp until hard

pin and glue

Fig 6/6 *Elementary open-top construction. The inset sketch shows how the cross brace is notched to take the road.*

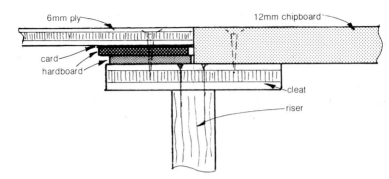

Fig 6/7 *Compensating for differing thicknesses of sub-base.*

as shown in Fig 6/7. It will be found more convenient if the joints are arranged, as shown, over one of the supports. Although I've shown the track bases as having gentle curves, this is by no means essential. Indeed, if you don't have a power jig-saw, and have to shape the base the hard way with a pad-saw, only those track bases forming the top of embankments need to be cut to a smooth curve, the rest can be sawn in straight lines.

In the immediate post-war period, new timber was completely unobtainable and so we made our baseboards out of anything we could lay our hands on. Although this is no longer necessary, the methods we developed are just as applicable today. Fig 6/8 shows a corner section built entirely from odd bits of timber, plywood and hardboard. Note how the backscenes form part of the framing. One doesn't normally associate hardboard with framing, but suitably braced, with, I suggest, timber of about 20 mm square section, it is quite effective. This type of construction calls for a little experience in carpentry, and a modicum of ingenuity. Baseboard sizes do however tend to depend on the size of available timber.

Up to now, I've assumed a sectional layout, indeed there is a body of opinion that claims that all layouts should be built in sections so that, should you ever move, the line can be easily re-erected in the new home. It is a very plausible theory, but in the many moves I have made over my life, I've never found the new site to be anything like the old in size or shape! There are advantages and disadvantages to building the layout *in situ*, but, where economy is the watchword a fixed baseboard tends to be the cheaper of the two. There are indeed, two highly economical approaches available for a permanent layout.

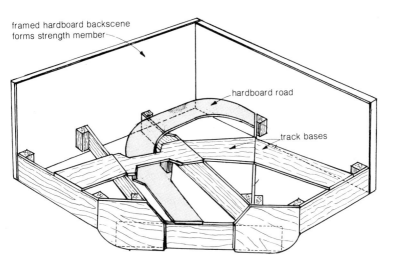

framed hardboard backscene
forms strength member

hardboard road

track bases

Above Fig 6/8 *Open-top corner section built from short lengths of material.*

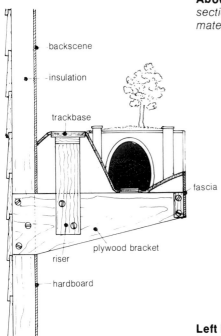

backscene

insulation

trackbase

fascia

plywood bracket

riser

hardboard

Left Fig 6/9 *Simple framing for use in garden shed.*

Fig 6/10 *Baseboard framing in loft.*

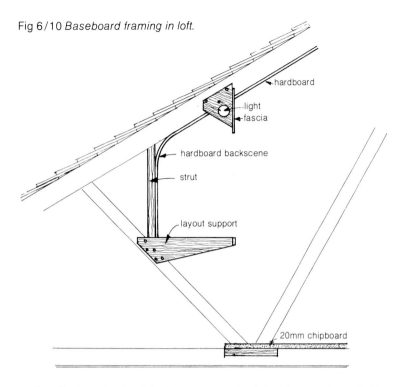

The first works best in the garden shed, but is equally suitable anywhere where you can drill and plug the walls for the brackets. The idea is to screw cantilever frames, of not less than 9 mm thickness, to the vertical timbers of the shed. Fig 6/9 shows such an arrangement in cross section. The important thing is to have the front drop not less than 35 mm, and the angle at around 15°, thus ensuring that the rear bracket is proportional in depth to the overhang, which should not exceed 500 mm and is ideally kept to between 200 and 350 mm. The track bases, which should be from 9 to 12 mm thick, brace the brackets sideways, so only a very thin fascia board is needed along the front, mainly for appearance! For station areas, the base material will cover the entire area, but as there is, in practice, no front frame, the edge may be curved. This arrangment, the soft edge, produces a very pleasing effect to the eye. Needless to say, this type of construction is extremely effective on scenic sections, as there is ample scope for the landscape to vary in profile to any degree required.

In the loft, a substantially similar approach is feasible, though the size of the bracket tends to be rather larger, due to the angles of the roof timbers. Modern lofts, with factory made principals are, if anything, more amenable to this sort of treatment, though on the other hand, you do get a lot of cross timbers where you don't want them — around your feet! Fig 6/10 shows a possible arrangement. Note the provision of a lighting fascia, it is simple, yet highly effective.

The other recommended arrangement for a permanent site is the 'L' girder system, developed largely by Linn Westcott of the *Model Railroader*. In the original version, heavy timber was used — in the USA, wood is relatively cheap. In practice, you can get away with much thinner material than was originally specified, though with the

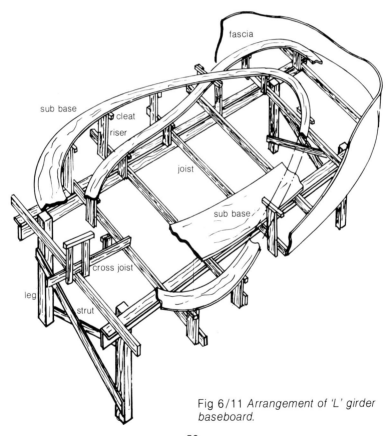

Fig 6/11 *Arrangement of 'L' girder baseboard.*

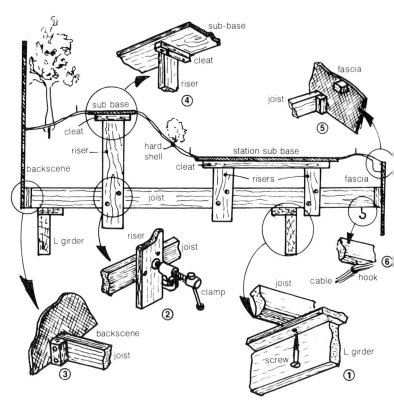

Fig 6/12 *Details of 'L' girder construction.* **1** *The 'L' girder is made from two lengths of wood glued and pinned. Joists are screwed from underneath.* **2** *Risers are held temporarily with a clamp whilst gradients are adjusted.* **3** *The backscene and fascia boards are screwed to small cleats.* **4** *Top of riser, showing cleat.* **5** *Small wood blocks on fascia provide anchorage for landscape.* **6** *Cable runs can be supported on hooks.*

'L' girder arrangement, the depth of the main girder is dependent on the span between the legs. I'd suggest a depth of 75 mm with a thickness of 12 mm for spans up to 2 m. Fig 6/11 shows a typical 'L' girder structure, whilst the various parts are shown in greater detail in Fig 6/12. It is very much a catch-as-catch can system, for the great advantage lies in the fact that with 'L' girder construction, you do not need timber of a uniform size. The risers and cleats can be made from odds and ends, the joists can be any timber of

Above *Simple 'L' girder construction utilizing varying sections of timber.*

Below *Multi-level construction. It can be seen that the timber is of varying section—every bit was an offcut from a scrapbox.*

reasonable size that will span the gap. There is just one vital point to bear in mind, the distance between the joists need to be longer than your screwdriver, otherwise you are going to have a lot of trouble screwing the cleats in place. In this location, Posidrive screws are preferable.

One advantage of an 'L' girder structure lies in the fact that all screws can be inserted from underneath. This makes it a fairly straightforward buisness to alter alignment of levels, as you can get underneath to make the necessary adjustments. Of course, it then becomes necessary to alter part of the landscape — which is a very good reason for making sure your tracks are as you want them before you construct the scenery.

As long as the two 'L' girder tops are level, you do the rest of the setting up as you go along. Although this has little to do with economy — except of effort — I should point out that for permanent baseboard construction, the most essential measuring instrument

More multi-level construction, again small lengths of light timber are employed to support the track base.

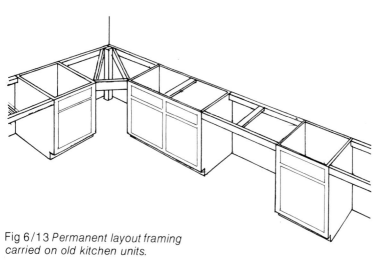

Fig 6/13 *Permanent layout framing carried on old kitchen units.*

is a good long spirit level. Do not use a rule for this purpose — the floor is rarely a true level surface!

Baseboards need support, and legs tend to cost money. It's not, perhaps, appreciated that a good deal of the necessary support may be to hand. One aspect of our modern society is that second-hand furniture is something of a drug on the market. I'm not, of course, talking about the choicer items, for clearly, if you happen to own some really good furniture, you tend to cherish it. It's the cheaper stuff, in particular, the pack-flat chipboard items that are almost impossible to dispose of. Old, discarded kitchen units, in particular, are often thrown away, yet a selection of these makes a very good foundation for a permanent model railway. The worktops need to be removed, the sink can be discarded, and then the various units may be placed strategically around the railway room, with gaps bridged by odd lengths of timber as shown in Fig 6/13.

Although kitchen units are very convenient, since they provide a range of supports of identical height, almost any discarded cabinet, chest, bookcase and so on, is equally useful under the baseboard. Although it may be the wrong height, with stuff that was heading for the scrapheap you can get to work with a saw and make drastic changes. Furniture is not only an invaluable source of good solid support, it also provides a home for a mass of modelling material and somewhere to store the host of household items you don't need but which are too good to throw out. And, of course, it is just as suitable for supporting a sectional layout as it is as an integral part of a permanent system.

SAVINGS WITH TRACK

Trackwork is the largest single item of the railway model proper and is therefore the area where the diligent budget-conscious modeller can make appreciable savings since the sheer quantity of track involved makes any economy in this quarter quite marked. Admitedly, the use of ready-made track of one form or another is very convenient, and I would refer the reader back to the first chapter where I analysed the pros and cons of home trackbuilding. If you build your own track, you are taking on a major project. I don't want to over-emphasize the work involved, for the trackwork of the largest 4 mm scale layout I know of, Jim Savage's magnificent EM gauge model of the GWR in Somerset, was entirely built by the owner. As it reproduces not only Taunton station, but most of the adjacent stations as well, as they were in the latter days of steam and with every item of main line pointwork accurately modelled, it is a rather large model. Whilst the track alone took Jim the whole of five years spare time, this is exceptional. For the majority of model railways, six months to a year's concentrated effort should suffice while, if the layout is being built in stages, the fact that tracklaying alternates with other facets of the hobby makes the task quite pleasant.

Small scale track construction traditionally involves soldering and also requires the construction of a few jigs. Track gauges are required, they can be purchased or constructed at home. The fact that many commercial gauges appear to require machine tools is simply a reflection of the difference between commercial and private resources. Probably the most convenient home-made gauge is the simple gauge block, a piece of wood which has been precisely cut to the chosen gauge along its width. A gauge lath, which is required for certain jigs, is merely a long strip, again cut precisely to gauge. This is where a precision saw bench is a great convenience, but hand work is not too difficult. I prefer to use 3 or 4 mm ply for gauge blocks and laths.

The most popular home-construction system in use today employs printed circuit board (PCB) sleepers, which are suitably gapped for two-rail insulation, to which the rails are soldered directly. It is a very good system with great advantages where pointwork is concerned, but cost-wise there is at best a marginal saving over the cost of plain track. Nevertheless, there is a saving and moreover, one does get a choice of rail section. This is an area where economy goes hand in hand with appearance. Soldered

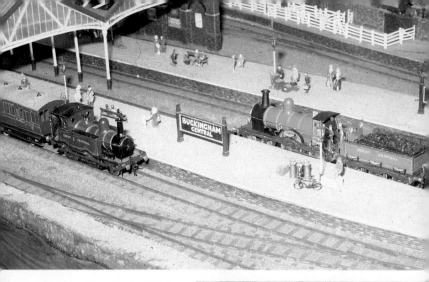

Above 'Buckingham Central', Peter Denny's superb 4 mm scale evocation of Edward England. This model has been built up, on a strict budget, over some forty years. Standing on the nearest platform road is a local train headed by a Sacre 'Altrincham' 2-4-0T, whilst a Sacre 4-4-0 runs into the centre road at the head of a semi-fast train. Both locomotives, and virtually everything else in this picture, were built by Peter Denny.

Right A mixed gauge on Mike Sharman's mid-Victorian extravaganza. The four-wheeled tipper wagons run on Brunel's magnificent 7 ft gauge metals, a standard gauge loco shunts the smaller chaldron wagons at the end of the new spur. Note the baulk road 'under construction' and the early steam shovel in the background.

Left *This detail shot of a Continental branch model shows how effective well conceived scenery can be. The landscape, made from plaster, carefully painted, is the main ingredient and this costs very little in cash.*

Below *A selection of low-relief scratchbuilt models provide a townscape on the Macclesfield MRC's 4 mm scale layout. Many of the small fittings are low-cost commercial items that add enormously to the scene's effectiveness.*

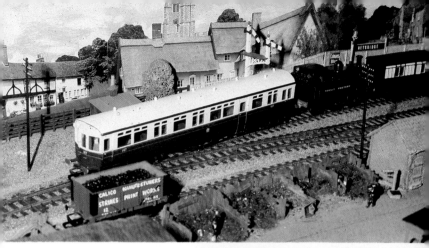

Bottom left *A small goods yard on the Macclesfield MRC's 'Botley Town' layout. The majority of the lineside fittings and structures can be easily scratchbuilt at little or no cost, turning what might be a fairly blank scene into a busy, interesting model.*

Above *Heybridge Station on the Macclesfield MRC's GWR layout. The backscene is a pleasing combination of low-relief models and a printed scene from a large calendar, which, twelve months on, cost absolutely nothing!*

Above right *This small weighbridge house on Alan Wright's 'Inglenook Sidings' is an excellent subject for an initial essay in building construction.*

Right *Dave Pennington's 'Stanmore', an accurate model of the now defunct LNWR branch that used to run from Harrow and Wealdstone on the West Coast main line. All buildings are scratchbuilt replicas of the prototype structures, depicting the line's heyday in the early years of the century.*

Above *Narrow gauge modelling, which involves a small stud of locos and short trains, running in delightful scenery is one low-cost approach to an unusual model railway. This model, by The Cardiff MRC, is typical of the better work in this genre.*

Below *Henblas Farm on Dave Rowe's first extension to the original 'Milkwood' scene, a marvellous piece of pure modelmaking.*

Scratchbuilt soldered track on Peter Denny's second 'Buckingham' layout.

track in 4 mm scale, using scale section bullhead rail, will accept all current ready-to-run flanges, since there are no fixings on the inside of the rail. Nickel silver is not cheap, and a 30 per cent reduction in the amount of metal used does effect a very real economy, and, at the same time, produces a more realistic track. It isn't often appreciated that one reason EM and P4 look better than OO is that most OO layouts use code 100 rail, which is somewhat overscale, particularly for a steam-age model. EM and P4 models invariably employ scale section rail, and whilst it is none too easy to be absolutely positive over the gauge, particularly from the usual position (broadside on to the track), it is easy to spot the difference in the height of the rail!

For the straightforward assembly of PCB track, you need a track jig, as in Fig 7/1, to ensure that your sleepers are correctly spaced.

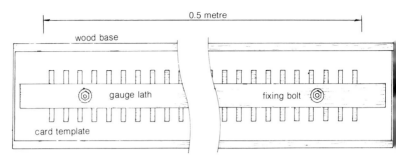

Above Fig 7/1 *Jig for making PCB track.*

Below *Jig for assembling PCB sleepered track.*

Bottom *Close up of PCB sleeper track assembly jig.*

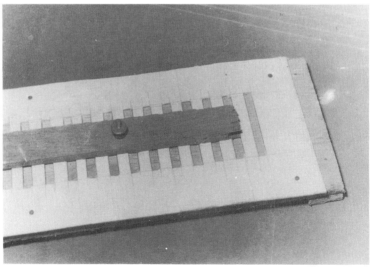

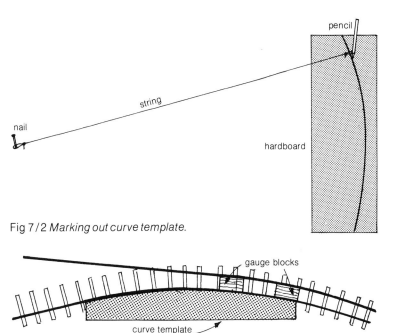

Fig 7/2 *Marking out curve template.*

Fig 7/3 *Using template to construct curved PCB track.*

This consists of a thin mask, usually made from card around 1 mm thick, in which a series of slots is cut to take the sleepers. It is not difficult to make, in fact I put two together in a couple of hours, though I admit that having a good drawing board does simplify the marking out, particularly as both masks were marked out together. The jig should be slightly over 0.5 m in length, and secured to a piece of wood or chipboard. A gauge lath is then bolted down the centre of the jig.

In use, the gauge lath is removed and sleepers inserted in the jig. The gauge lath is then replaced and bolted down and one length of rail is soldered in place against the gauge lath. For straight track you now solder the second rail in place against the gauge lath before removing the lath and track from the jig.

If curved track is required, the gauge lath is taken away, the 'half track' removed and placed safely on a suitable surface (not the floor!). You now need a curve template. These are available for 16.5 and 9 mm gauges, and very nice they are, but long before they become available, I made my own from hardboard. Fig 7/2 shows how to mark out the curve with a length of looped string and a pencil. In practice, the precise radius can be achieved by wrapping several turns of string around the pencil and unrolling as you go along. You now place the 'half track' against the template, as shown in Fig 7/3, and solder the second rail in place, using gauge blocks.

For maximum realism, your tracks should curve sinuously, not form a geometric succession of straights and curves. If the half track is laid *in situ* on the baseboard, it is possible to ease it into gently flowing curves before the second rail is soldered into place. Clearly, this will be the nearer of the two rails, since soldering on the back of the track is not that easy.

The only serious objection to PCB track is the cost of the individual sleepers, for whilst they are quite reasonably priced, you do need a lot — 100 sleepers to the metre in 4 mm scale. Cutting your own sleepering from sheet PCB is cheaper, but is only practicable if you have a reasonably powerful miniature circular sawbench, and so, for a complete low-cost system, we revert to an older form of two-rail construction, which is, of course, as good today as it was forty years ago. It has a marginal advantage in the use of real timber sleepers.

You need, initially, a supply of thin sheet wood — I'll come to this later — a steel straight edge, a small square and a stout trimming knife with a good sharp blade. A set of dividers can be useful, but a home-made marking out rule is equally effective. This latter comprises a suitable piece of material, ideally an old school-pattern wooden ruler with the divisions planed off one edge. This is then carefully marked into sleeper lengths, with an intermediate measure to denote the location of the 'chairs'. The requirements are

Fig 7/4 *Sleeper size and spacing, British track (see Table 7/1).*

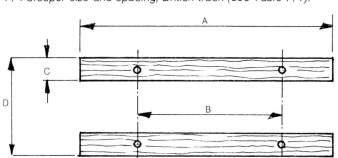

shown in Fig 7/4 with the dimensions for various requirements in the table below. You could, on the other side of the rule, set out the sleeper widths, but I personally prefer to use dividers for this purpose — which is fine if you have a set of dividers to hand.

Table 7/1   Sleeper dimensions

Gauge	A	B	C	D
OO	34(36)*	19	3	10
EM/P4	34(36)	20	3	10
TT	25.5(27)	14	2.25	7.5
N/2 mm	17(18)	11	1.5	5

All dimensions in mm. (The dimensions in brackets refer to the old 9 ft long sleeper and the modern 8 ft 6 in pattern.)
Length (A) shown thus — Modern 8 ft 6 in (Old 9 ft 0 in)
*Scale size: reduce by 1 mm to compensate for underscale gauge

Now to the timber. The best source of supply is a sheet of low-grade 3-ply wood. I stress low grade, because we want it to come apart. I discovered this feature by accident when a piece of tea-chest ply got soaked way back in the early '40s and proceeded to disintegrate. The three pieces of veneer separated easily, but instead of cursing, I realized I'd got a large amount of very thin wood. I soon found out how easy it was to cut it into individual sleepers. Failing a piece of otherwise tolerably useless plywood, you will have to go out and purchase veneer or 1 mm ply. However, I've an idea that a diligent search will not be in vain.

Take a section of veneer a little shorter than your straight edge and about as wide as the blade of your square, with the grain running parallel to the long edge. Carefully cut a true edge along the line of grain and with your sleeper-length rule, mark out sleepers and the position of the 'chairs', as in Fig 7/5. Then, placing the true edge along the side of your cutting board, and using your square, pencil firmly across along the 'chair' lines, then *half cut* through the wood at sleeper lengths. This is not too difficult, since the grain of the timber runs against the knife cut.

Now trim the material into sleeper widths using the straight edge and trimming knife, cutting along the grain. If you are using a single sheet of veneer, a single stroke with a sharp knife will usually do the trick. It only remains to break up the individual sleepers from the long strips and place them carefully into a box for future use. This is not a long-winded job, indeed, you'll probably find you can produce

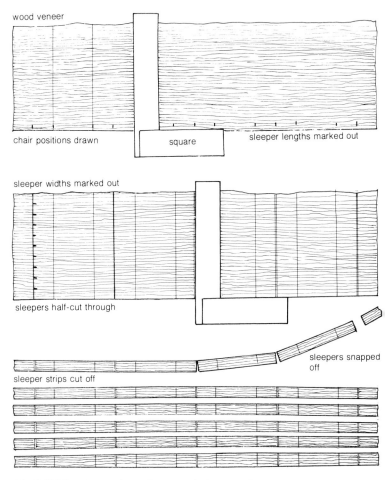

wood veneer

chair positions drawn

square

sleeper lengths marked out

sleeper widths marked out

sleepers half-cut through

sleepers snapped off

sleeper strips cut off

Fig 7/5 *The stages in cutting wood sleepers from veneer.*

a fair quantity of sleepers in far less time than it took me to write this out, let alone prepare the diagrams!

The next requirement is the 'chair'. I use $\frac{1}{4}$ in brass gimp pins, which are, I understand, still obtainable from upholsterers — if you can find one. My supply was bought some forty years ago, I got a $\frac{1}{4}$ lb box and have, so far, only used about half. As they come in handy for dozens of other purposes, you may get a fair idea just how many are in a large box. In practice, any short, flat-headed pin may be

74

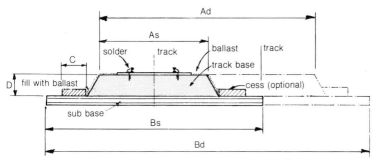

Fig 7/6 *Dimensions of track base and sub-base (see Table 7/2).*

used, and whilst I prefer brass, some people maintain that steel is better. I've seen some pins with blackened heads, but these only need a bit of work with a fine flat file to remove the coating.

You next require a track base. Fig 7/6 shows such a base in cross section and shows the most elaborate arrangement possible, with a semi-hardboard track base on a ply or hardboard sub-base. I've shown the cess, the narrow raised strip alongside the ballast, the inclusion of which, provides a very good model of prototype track. You can just stick to the track base proper, but the arrangement shown is strong enough to form a self-supporting member in an open top layout. The dimensions are given in the table below.

Table 7/2 Track base dimensions

Scale	A		B		C	D
	Single	Double	Single	Double		
7	90	175	150	250	18	9
4	50	100	90	140	10	9
3	50	75	70	100	7	6
2	25	50	45	70	5	6

All dimensions in mm.

Construction is shown in Fig 7/7. You need first to align the sleepers. I prefer to pencil in the outer lines, then place the sleepers individually using dividers for spacing — see Table 7/1 for this — but others prefer a 'comb' pattern spacing jig. The sleepers are generally glued down with PVA woodworking adhesive.

You now have to insert the 'chairs'. Here you have a choice. If you

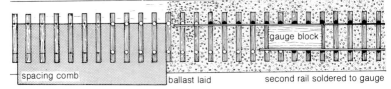

sleepers located, holes pierced and gimp pins driven in   first rail soldered in place

gauge block

spacing comb   ballast laid   second rail soldered to gauge

Above Fig 7/7 *Constructing soldered track using wooden sleepers.*

Below *Sleeper spacing comb for wooden-sleepered track.*

Bottom *Sample of soldered track using wooden sleepers and gimp pins. The track base is made from 9 mm thick Sundeala semi-hard insulation board, the sub-base is 6 mm ply.*

own a small 12 v electric drill, you simply drill small holes into the sleeper and track base, but failing this a sharp bradawl is just as effective. If you split a sleeper, remove and replace it. You may, as I do, prefer to pin rather than glue the sleepers down — this does make replacement a shade easier. You need a fairly light cross-pein hammer and will probably find a pair of fine tweezers essential for holding the pins in place.

Once the pins are in place, it is a good idea to rub the top surface smooth with a fine file and this is essential if you are using blackened pins. Beware of removing the head completely! If you are forced to use long pins, which protrude below the track base, the best arrangement is to invert the track base over a block of metal — the sole of a discarded electric iron is ideal — and tap the underside flat with a hammer. This should be done before polishing the heads and, furthermore, assumes a fair projection below the base. A small projection only needs to be filed smooth.

Now apply the ballast. You need a moderately broad brush which fits neatly between the sleepers, and some PVA woodworking adhesive let down with about a quarter of its bulk with water. Coat the base between the sleepers liberally, and then give the edges of the track base a final thick coat. Place on a sheet of newspaper and cover deeply with ballast, place another sheet of newspaper on top and then press the ballast firmly into the adhesive. Leave overnight to set. The following evening, remove your ballasted lengths and return the surplus ballast to the container.

A word about ballast: you can purchase this from various sources, and every writer has his own pet preference. I am, perhaps, an exception, I've tried most and with one horrible exception (which I didn't even consider worth trying), consider them all to be completely satisfactory. The exception is birdseed — it looks fine until various pests discover you've laid out a delicious feast for them! This is bad enough, but they've been known to turn to the rest of the model after exhausting the ballast. Chicken grit, dried coffee grounds, fine sieved stone chippings, cork dust are all very good. If there happens to be a quarry or a stonemasons near to hand, you can probably get hold of a large amount of dust for the bother of collecting the stuff; the main difficulty lies in persuading the foreman that you aren't crazy!

You now have your sub-base, laid with sleepers into which small chairs are driven, suitably ballasted. You just solder the rail in place, using track gauges to ensure accuracy. Incidentally, I still use what I have always preferred, a short block of wood, about 30 mm long for

The track on 'Leasingthorne' is entirely scratchbuilt—the excellent effect can be gauged from this photograph.

OO gauge, cut to precisely 16.5 mm in width. Metal gauges, used in close proximity to a hot soldering iron, tend to get hot themselves and whilst the expansion is neither here nor there, you need to move them around. Believe me, moving a metal gauge that has had a soldering iron close to it for any time at all is something you don't do twice with your bare fingers. A wood gauge, on the other hand, remains comfortable to hold, and lasts for quite a long while before it gets too charred to be accurate.

As gimp pins may prove difficult to obtain, Fig 7/8 shows an alternative, using short plated, office pins. These are pushed through the sleepers into the track base, using a small pair of pliers. The pins are then cut short with a pair of side cutters, preferably using a slip of card about 0.75 mm thick to get the height uniform. After that, the rails are just soldered in place.

Soldered track built in this fashion is reasonably realistic — a lot depends on the sort of solder 'blob' you get on each 'chair', this is one of those jobs where practice makes perfect. This form of construction is primarily intended for bullhead track — the more modern flat-bottom rail can be spiked directly to the sleepers, as in

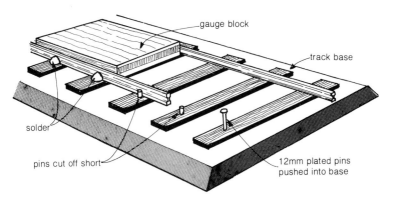

Fig 7/8 *Construction of track using small office pins.*

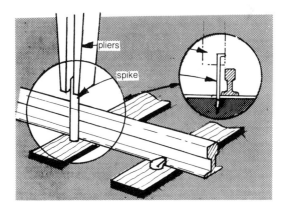

Fig 7/9 *Construction of spiked track using flat bottom rail.*

Fig 7/9. The spikes are simply pushed home with a small pair of flat-nosed pliers, and here it is essential to use Sundeala or similar semi-hard insulation board for the track base.

Home-built track on a sub-base is quite cheap and very versatile, since it is, in a sense, sectional track, and can be lifted and relaid several times before it begins to show serious signs of wear and tear. Moreover, where it is sandwiched onto a thin ply base a shade wider than the track base proper, as I suggest, you get a good sub-base for open top construction, and so you don't need a baseboard surface at all. And that is a very real saving indeed!

CONSTRUCTING POINTWORK

The greatest single economy on any model railway comes from building the pointwork. A home-built turnout costs less than a quarter the price of the most inexpensive commercial product, and that is only the start. Commercial points are always built as individual units to give the purchaser the greatest flexibility in use, whilst allowing the manufacturer to spread the extremely high tooling costs over the maximum number of units. Home-made

Soldered pointwork under construction on the Model Railway Club's 'New Annington' 00 gauge layout.

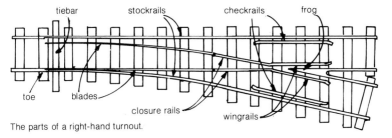

The parts of a right-hand turnout.

Fig 8/1 *The parts of a standard turnout.*

turnouts can be tailor-made for the job, and simply by making an entire station throat in one unit, you can save anything up to 10 per cent in length. Furthermore, given only a little care, you can make turnouts which are superior to all but the very best, and most expensive, commercial products.

As a result, there are many individuals who, whilst using a commercial flexible track to save a lot of tedious work, build their own pointwork to match. Indeed, there are a couple of specialized 4 mm scale flexible track systems that have no matching turnouts, and the combination of ready-built track and home-made turnouts is a very sound one where it isn't absolutely necessary to watch every copper. It makes best use of your time, and cuts out a good deal of tedium.

First of all, let's look at the parts of a standard turnout (shown in Fig 8/1). The various parts are labelled and we shall be using these terms throughout. One important feature that needs to be noted is that, as in prototype practice, one uses the angle of the turnout rather than its 'radius' — radii are only quoted for toy train set tracks, and then solely as a matter of convenience. Furthermore, the angle is quoted as a number, not in degrees, the number giving the ratio of the angle. Thus, a 'No 8' turnout, the largest normally employed in model form, has an angle produced by setting out eight units along the straight centre line and one unit at right angles to this. The

Fig 8/2 *Turnout angles.*

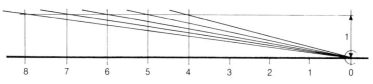

Left Fig 8/3 *First stage in turnout construction: stockrails laid, with joggles correctly aligned. Note that the tiebar is already in place.*

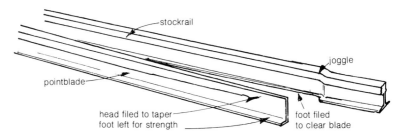

stockrail

joggle

pointblade

head filed to taper
foot left for strength

foot filed
to clear blade

Above Fig 8/4 *Detail of point blade and joggle.*

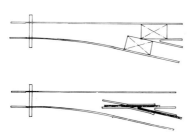

Left Fig 8/5 *The second stage in turnout construction: using gauge blocks to get the 'V' of the frog in the correct position.*

Left Fig 8/6 *The third stage of turnout construction: aligning wingrails and closure rails.*

angled centre line is then drawn from the tip of this projection to the origin of the eight units. Fig 8/2 shows the more common angles employed.

A No 6 turnout is a good general purpose design for main line usage. A No 4 turnout is about the sharpest you should use, and then only on industrial railways or in goods yards. Narrow gauge lines often employ No 4 turnouts, but once again, a No 5 or No 6 is better. The No 8 turnout is generally used only on high class layouts, where a small sacrifice in length is counterbalanced by the improvement in appearance. It is also worth pointing out (no pun intended!) that the larger the number, the better running you will get, simply because you aren't throwing the rolling stock about quite so abruptly. This is particularly important where steam-age modelling is concerned, for model locomotive bogies and pony trucks are particularly susceptible to derailment on suspect track. Diesel-era stock, running on double bogies, can cope much more easily with indifferent trackwork.

The initial requirement is a full-sized diagram of the turnout. You can buy these — in general, specialist societies such as the EM Gauge Society are the best source — or you can draw it out yourself. If you do so, make a final drawing in black ink on tracing paper, in this way both right and left-hand drawings can be produced from the one original in a photocopier.

If you are producing a complete track assembly — as shown in the photographs — then you arrange the point plans on a piece of sheet material. I prefer ply, but anything will do. When all is in place, you secure them down with short bits of sticky tape. The next step is to cut the sleepers to length from PCB sleeper strip, using a small hacksaw. Now lay some double-sided sticky tape along the centre of the point and press the PCB sleepering in place.

The next job is to solder one stock-rail in place as in Fig 8/3. However, before you do this, put in the joggle for the point blade to sit into. This can be filed, but I prefer to kink the rail, using a pair of pliers. There is a knack to this, so practice carefully on a scrap length of rail. Fig 8/4 shows the arrangement with flat-bottom track, where some extra work is involved.

When the first stock rail is in place, you repeat the process with the second. Now you need two wooden gauge blocks. These are jammed together as shown in Fig 8/5 to form the 'V' of the frog. You now need to file two pieces of rail to fit this 'V', which again is easy once you've got the knack of it. The two lengths of rail are then soldered in place, and the gauge blocks removed.

We now come to the tricky bit. The wingrail has to be bent to the correct angle at a position where the end of the blade fits the joggle when the wingrail is correctly spaced and the closure rail is *exactly* in line with the frog. You now need two slips of aluminium as thick as the checkrail clearance — this is, for OO, 1 mm. For other gauges, check your table of standards. The wingrails are now laid, using two of these gauges, as shown in Fig 8/6.

Now you have to file the point blades from the rail. This is often put forward as a very difficult business, but as always, there is a straightforward method you can use. Take a length of flat mild steel about 100 mm long and clamp it horizontally in the vice. Now, at one end, clamp a length of rail as shown in Fig 8/7. With the rail firmly supported on the metal, and held equally firmly in place, you file *away* from the clamp, lifting the file off the rail on the return stroke, or else you'll buckle the rail and ruin the job. You continue filing until you have a neat taper about 30 mm long, ending in a feather edge. The other face needs a slightly less fine taper so that, at the very

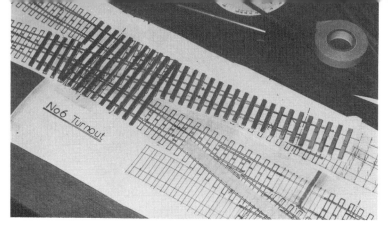

Top *Soldered pointwork, using PCB sleepering, under construction 1: point plans fixed to temporary base, double sided adhesive tape laid down and PCB sleepering fixed in position.*

Above *Soldered pointwork, using PCB sleepering, under construction 2: stockrails soldered in place on prepared PCB sleepering.*

Below *Soldered pointwork, using PCB sleepering, under construction 3: close-up showing rails being gauged with roller type gauge, an alternative to the wooden gauge block.*

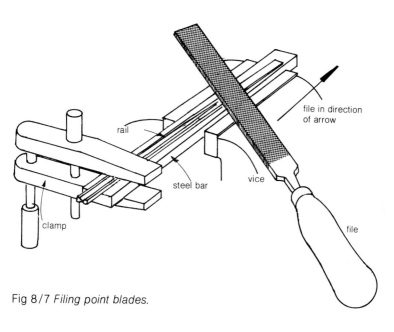

Fig 8/7 *Filing point blades.*

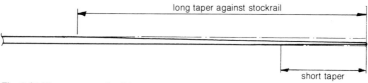

Fig 8/8 *Taper on point blade.*

Fig 8/9 *Final stage in turnout construction: point blades and checkrails installed.*

end, you are down to something below the thickness of the central web of the rail. Fig 8/8 shows this in practice. Again, it's a job that is easy once you've acquired the knack. Note I don't say skill, this is not high precision filing by any means!

You need two point blades, of opposite hands. I prefer to file up a batch at a time, since getting the tools together and setting up the job takes more time than filing away the metal. The blades are put in place as in Fig 8/9, which also shows the checkrails going in. Here you use the spacing slips mentioned above to ensure the correct

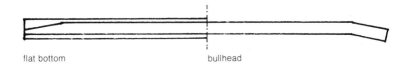

flat bottom   bullhead

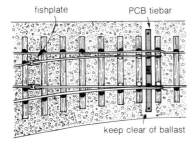

fishplate   PCB tiebar

keep clear of ballast

Above Fig 8/10 *Detail of checkrail.*

Left Fig 8/11 *Detail of toe of point, showing the pivoting of the point blades.*

Below Fig 8/12 *Detail of tiebar.*

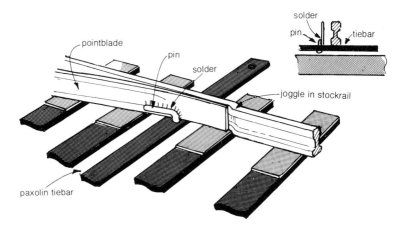

gap is maintained. The ends of bullhead checkrails and wingrails are bent, but, as Fig 8/10 shows, with flat bottom rail, the rail is machined on the prototype and filed on the model. You need to give flexibility to the point blades — which is quite easy if you simply connect them with a small fishplate as shown in Fig 8/11.

I've not mentioned the tiebar. There are several schools of thought, and once again, it is largely a matter of choice. One method employs thin plastic sheet and small pins. Fig 8/12 explains the principle, this arrangement is essential where the point blades are integral with the closure rails, as it provides flexibility. Where the

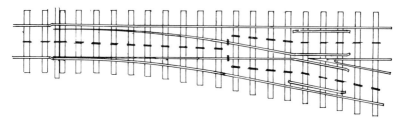

Fig 8/13 *Gapping of PCB sleepers for two-rail electrification.*

blades are separate — the easier arrangement, in my opinion — you will, by using a shortened rail joiner or a true fishplate to connect the blade to the closure rail, have made a reasonable facsimilie of the prototype joint, and so can use a sleeper, reduced in width by some 30 per cent, to form an excellent tiebar.

The final task is to introduce the necessary breaks in the PCB surface for two-rail insulation. Fig 8/13 shows how to arrange these. Note that there needs to be a gap in the closure rail, which is generally cut with a fine saw after assembly is complete and the finished turnout is removed from the board. I admit to have skated quickly over the method of gapping. It is feasible to do all this with a razor saw, or a riffler file, but my preference is a small abrasive disc in a miniature 12 v drill, worked from the power supply. To round off electrical matters, Fig 8/14 shows how the frog is energized by means of a small changeover switch coupled to the tiebar, details of which come in the following chapter.

Although I've dealt with PCB sleepers, a similar arrangement can be used to build pointwork with wood sleepers and gimp-pin 'chairs'. You need to mark out your track base very carefully, and so,

Fig 8/14 *Two-rail turnout wiring.*

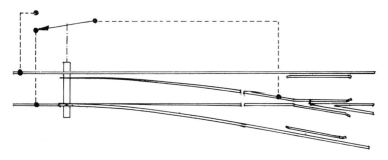

Fig 8/15 *Track gauge for point jig. Key:* **A**—*intersection of angle;* **X**—*locating holes.*

if you prefer to draw out the track onto the ply, then by all means do so. Otherwise, proceed as before, with one important variation, the point plans are firmly glued down onto the track base, as you will, subsequently, be ballasting over them.

The only other difference lies in the need to mark out the locations of the 'chairs', and then to drill the necessary holes. I could go into a long-winded description, but I'm tolerably certain that, once you've got the sleepers down in place, it will be completely obvious where the pins will go.

I cannot over-emphasize the need to take care when constructing turnouts. It is absolutely vital that the checkrail and wingrail clearances are accurate, that the correct gauge is maintained throughout and that the closure rails are precisely aligned with the frog. I find that, in addition to the wooden track gauge blocks, a metal gauge is required to check gauge and clearances. I still use a Rogergauge, a device produced in the 1950s by a long defunct firm and never reintroduced since. The roller pattern gauge is readily available, and is very convenient — perhaps I'm just being ultra-conservative.

There is an alternative method of point construction, which is excellent if you are prepared to make a fairly elaborate jig and then largely confine yourself to one pattern of turnout. The jig is actually very simple in design, not too difficult to make, and, once made, will serve you indefinitely — providing you don't lose it! You just require

Fig 8/16 *Filing to 'split the dots'.*

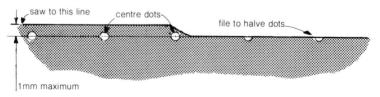

a supply of sheet aluminium around 1 mm thick, some simple tools, a little patience and a lot of determination.

The first part of the jig, the track gauge, is shown in Fig 8/15. It must be made with care, for on it the entire accuracy of the turnout depends, as it locates the stock-rails and the 'V' of the frog. You begin by setting out one straight centre line, then from this you set the turnout angle. This is where the advantage of using the prototype ratio rather than the model degree is immediately advantageous, it's relatively easy to lay out a 1 in 6 or 1 in 5 angle.

You now put a line of centre pop marks along both centre lines and scribe lightly across at right angles to the centre line. With a pair of dividers set precisely at half your chosen gauge, strike off the gauge on each cross line, and then add centre dots. Now fair in the curve. Mark the outer lines with centre punch marks at about 20 mm spacing.

You now cut carefully to the line. Well, if you're used to metal work, you do, but as the art of splitting centre-dots with a hacksaw takes a good deal of practice, you may prefer to play safe and cut about half a millimetre away. You now file to the line, making sure each centre dot is split in half as in Fig 8/16. This is an old workshop dodge, and is the best way of filing precisely to a line.

You ought to check both the flatness of the straight side and the accuracy of your gauge. The former is done with a straight-edge, or a good metal rule, the latter is done with calipers. The inexpensive caliper gauge is just about accurate enough for OO gauge and EM, but for 18.83 mm gauge you need a good vernier. The same applies to 2 mm scale, and to an extent, to N gauge as well, since the tolerances here are very small.

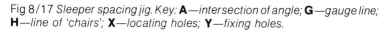

Fig 8/17 *Sleeper spacing jig. Key:* **A**—*intersection of angle;* **G**—*gauge line;* **H**—*line of 'chairs';* **X**—*locating holes;* **Y**—*fixing holes.*

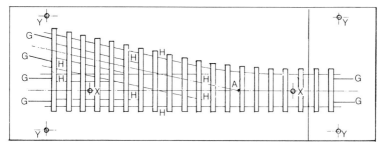

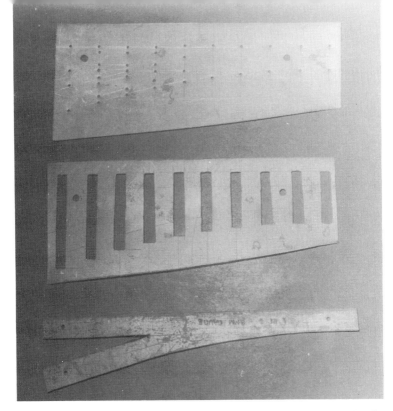

Aluminium jigs for constructing points. From top to bottom: overlay for drilling holes for 'chairs' in wooden sleepers, spacing jig for sleepers, track gauge jig. This jig is for a 4 mm scale, 9 mm gauge turnout (009), and can be used for either left or right hand turnouts by inverting the jigs.

Now comes the most tedious part of the job, making the main base, Fig 8/17. Using the gauge template described above, mark out the base, taking care that the sleeper markings are parallel and evenly spaced. Slots are cut for the sleepers. This is the sort of job where the advantages of a power drill become obvious, since the simplest method is to mark out a line of holes along the centre of each sleeper, and to drill out about 80 per cent of the metal. Fig 8/18 shows the correct technique, first you drill out alternate holes so that when you put the intermediate holes in, you don't drift off into the adjacent hole. After that, it's a matter of careful work with a succession of files. Four more securing holes are needed to allow you to fix the sleeper jig down.

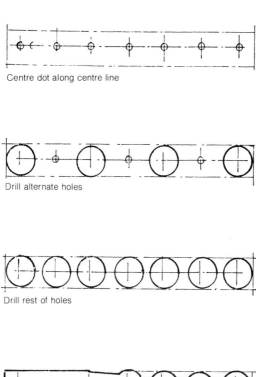

Centre dot along centre line

Drill alternate holes

Drill rest of holes

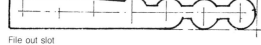

File out slot

Fig 8/18 *Stages in drilling and filing a slot.*

The photographs show a jig made for OO9 or HOe turnouts — in other words, 9 mm narrow gauge. In use, you align the sleeper jig on the sub-base, or, if you are constructing individual turnouts on PCB sleepering, you fix it to a piece of blockboard. Next, you insert the sleepers, cutting each to length from a section of sleepering. The procedure differs from this stage, according to the type of sleepering used.

Where PCB sleepers are used, you fix the sleeper jig to a piece of blockboard, insert the sleepers and secure them in place with the track gauge. Then you solder the outer rails in place and proceed as before, removing the track gauge when you have fixed the stock rails and frog. At the end, the whole turnout is carefully prised loose

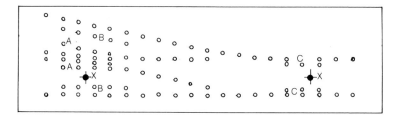

Fig 8/19 *Drilling jig for 'chairs'. Key:* **A***—wingrails;* **B***—checkrails;* **C***—slide-rails;* **X***—locating holes.*

and the next one is begun. To switch from right- to left-hand turnouts, you simply invert the jigs.

If you are using wood sleepers with pins, you first locate the sleeper jig, and screw it down. The sleepers are cut and fitted in place, and the track gauge secured over them. A line is penciled on either side, to locate the gimp pins, then the track gauge is removed and the small holes drilled as before. It would save a lot of time if you make another jig (Fig 8/19) to allow you to drill the holes without marking out first. After the gimp pins are driven home, remove the sleeper jig and secure the track gauge in place, taking care that the screws go back into the holes previously made.

It is clear that although you put a good deal of work into the manufacture of the jig in the first instance, once it is finished, your construction is greatly speeded up. Moreover, as the turnout is standardized, it is not too difficult to measure the lengths of rail needed, keep a note of the sizes and produce the necessary parts in small batches.

Before I leave the subject of pointwork, I should mention that every one of the specialist societies set up to foster a specific gauge provide instructions to members on tracklaying, often using components supplied by the society in question. The EM Gauge Society issue an excellent handbook, with a mass of information on both model and prototype track.

POINT AND SIGNAL CONTROL

The control of pointwork, and to a lesser extent, the operation of semaphore signals, is often considered to be one of the most expensive features of a model railway. This is because most modellers think of one method only — the commercial twin-solenoid point motor. There is no doubt that it is simple to use, and that it provides the most obvious practical system of remote control on a demountable table-top development of the basic ready-to-run train set, but it is only one of many systems available to the enthusiast working on a proper baseboard.

It isn't even the only electrically-operated system open to the modeller. I prefer relay operation, though I have to admit that I was fortunate enough, many years ago to come across a large supply of superb ex-US Navy relays which might have been made for the job in hand — at a bargain price. The GPO pattern 3000 type relay is also very highly regarded, and with the addition of a gain-stroke arm on the armature as shown in Fig 9/1, will operate a freely moving pair of point blades in 4 mm scale. If you can get hold of a supply of relays and are prepared to install the necessary dc power supply — which *must* be adequately smoothed with a choke-capacitor circuit, as detailed in Fig 9/2 — you can equip yourself with a very reliable system which allows you to add electrical detection, using the contacts on the relays. The system is easily controlled by simple, and relatively inexpensive on-off or wafer switches. Alas, with the growth of solid-state circuitry, the supply of cheap ex-

Fig 9/1 *Relay operation of turnout.*

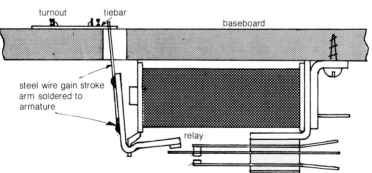

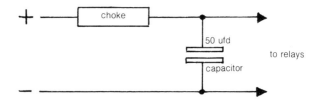

Fig 9/2 *Smoothing circuit for relay operation.*

equipment relays will inevitably dry up, indeed there are signs that it is already becoming somewhat difficult to get them.

Of course, there is one very straightforward solution — not to install remote control in the first place. On many layouts, most turnouts are within easy reach of the operator and so it is perfectly feasible to retain the simple point lever alongside the tiebar. However, quite apart from the lack of realism involved, if cost is the first consideration, this is not the cheapest solution as point levers cost money.

The oldest, simplest and in many ways, the best mechanical method of operating points remains the cycle spoke. It is, in case you have forgotten, a length of high quality steel rod, dead straight, with a small screwed nipple at one end and a bent-over end at the other (that bit we don't want, so it's sawn off). The rest of the spoke goes under the baseboard, passing through holes drilled in the framing, and runs directly under the tiebar. A simple wire loop (secured to the spoke with epoxy resin, with one end passing through a slot in the baseboard under the tiebar, and engaging in a small hole in the tiebar) provides the link between the rod and the point. The nipple is, of course, your operating knob. Figure 9/3 shows how it is arranged.

Of course, this simple system doesn't give you a 'centralized' control, but on the majority of small layouts, all the knobs will be within easy reach of the operator. A cycle spoke costs about 15p,

Fig 9/3 *Operating turnout with cycle spoke.*

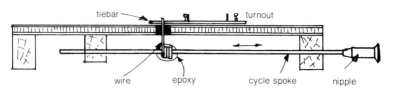

94

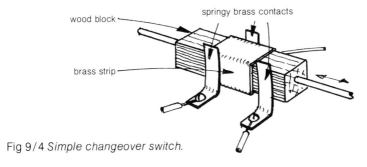

Fig 9/4 *Simple changeover switch.*

but if that stretches the budget, wire coathangers are the next best thing. They are stiff enough, but you will probably have some trouble straightening them out.

You can add electrical contacts. A simple system (Fig 9/4) involves a block of wood, about 8 mm square and about 20 mm long, with a narrow band of brass wrapped round it. Simple springy brass contacts screwed to the underside of the track base can form a crude, but reasonably effective changeover switch. This system is cheap, but only works reliably if you are very careful with the construction.

A more reliable, but naturally, more costly arrangement is to use a microswitch. These are totally enclosed change-over switches which are operated by a very small movement of a plunger. You secure the microswitch to the underside of the baseboard, arrange for a block of wood on the spoke to depress the plunger (as in Fig 9/5) and then proceed to forget you ever fitted the device. The chances of a microswitch failing are infinitesimally small and as the failure of a changeover switch creates so many problems — and

Simple slider control for wire-in-tube point operation. The sliders also actuate microswitches used to change polarity of point frogs.

Fig 9/5 *Microswitch operation.*

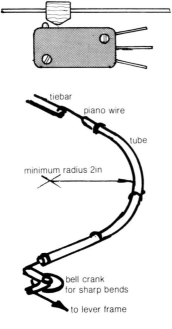

tiebar

piano wire

tube

minimum radius 2in

bell crank
for sharp bends

to lever frame

Fig 9/6 *Wire-in-tube operation.*

not a few headaches — this is one area where a relatively small expenditure is, I think, fully justified.

Another approach is the wire-in-tube system. Traditionally, you use piano wire passing through thin copper tube, but of late neoprene tubing has also been used. In effect, you use a bowden cable. The diagrams in Fig 9/6 explain the system, and I include a photo showing a simple slider that operates a microswitch for changing the polarity of the point frog. A substantially similar system has been used in the USA, based on car choke controls. Clearly, you don't throw the car away, instead, you go round to the local junk-yard and haggle. Regrettably, I've no information on the availability or cost in the UK.

If you want a proper lever frame, study Fig 9/7. This shows how it is possible to build up a system out of oddments of sheet metal, wire, woodscrews and, in particular, a supply of coil springs. This system, which to some extent follows the principles laid down by the late lamented Heath Robinson, works on a system of differential springing, a light tension spring beyond the point rocker, a heavier one in the pull wire. The idea is to keep the whole system in tension.

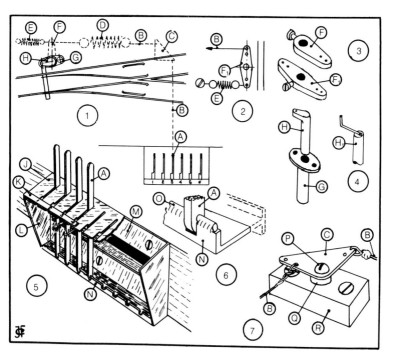

Fig 9/7 *Home-made lever frame.*

Key: **1** *Plan of system, operating wires shown dotted (beneath baseboard).*
2 *Arrangement of double crank where pivot is close to baseboard member.*
3 *Detail of bottom crank.* **4** *Pivot arm and tube.* **5** *Leverframe assembly.*
6 *Pivot arrangements for levers.* **7** *Detail of bellcrank.*

A—*point lever;* **B**—*pull-wire;* **C**—*bell crank;* **D**—*heavy spring;* **E**—*light
spring;* **F**—*bottom crank;* **F1**—*double crank;* **9**—*pivot tube;* **H**—*pivot arm;*
H1—*alternative pivot arm;* **J**—*level quadrant;* **K**—*stop bar soldered across
quadrant slots;* **L**—*side plates;* **M**—*back plate;* **N**—*bottom notched plate;*
O—*pivot rod soldered to notched plate;* **P**—*round-head woodscrew;*
Q—*thick washer;* **R**—*hardwood block.*

You need a fairly long movement on the point lever, as the heavy
spring does extend, but that is no great problem to arrange. The
various adjustment holes in the bell cranks allow for a good deal of
juggling to get each turnout to function properly. It's very effective,
but it does involve a good deal of careful adjustment to get it to work
— but on the other hand, once up and working it is fairly reliable.
    It is extremely difficult to take any mechanical system across the

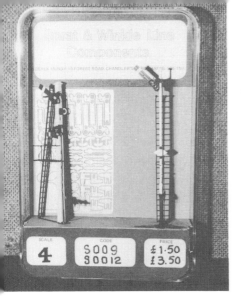

Left *4 mm scale upper quadrant signals built from 'Sprat and Winkle' kits.*

joints in a portable baseboard. I've seen several systems that worked, but I've also seen cases where the same system *didn't* work with any degree of reliability — and installing an unreliable remote control system is one of the quickest ways I know to kill all interest in the hobby. There is one very simple solution, you use two lever frames on either side of a baseboard joint and then add electrical remote control for those points on further sections. Alternatively, you can follow prototype practice and put in an extra lever frame. Many amateurs overlook the fact that prototype mechanical rodding has a limited range and that most large stations had a signalbox at each end.

In the early days of the hobby, twine was often used for point and signal control — mostly the latter. It lost favour because the best thread available was just not up to the job. Today, nylon thread is easily obtainable and the main problem — that of variable length as humidity alters — is overcome. I'm not, however going to describe the system in any detail because Ratio provide all the parts at a very reasonable cost, and add excellent instructional diagrams. The Ratio lever unit is reasonably priced and well worth considering for mechanical control of both points and signals where the budget isn't stretched to the limit.

As the Ratio system was initially developed to operate their signals, this brings me, conveniently, to the subject of signals on the layout. Not to put too fine a point on it, most people leave signals to last, and even when they are fitted, don't bother to make them work.

Right *4 mm scale signal with home-made electro-magnet operation.*

Below *4 mm scale bracket signal operated by home-made solenoids.*

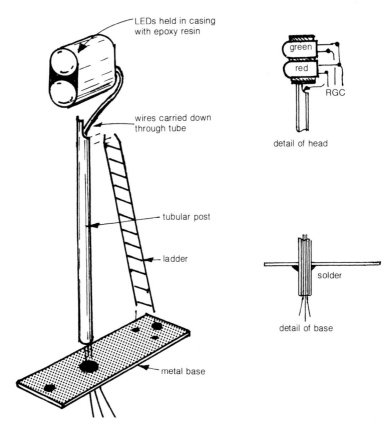

Fig 9/8 *Construction of simple colour light signal.*

This is rather a pity, because they do add enormously to the railway atmosphere. The simplest system is, without a doubt, colour-light signalling, and because these are compatable with late period main line steam as well as diesels, we'll begin here.

Colour lights are simple to operate, you only need wire and switches, plus a supply of electricity. They happen to be costly to purchase but they are relatively cheap to build. You need some small bore brass tube, some odd scrap, epoxy resin and either miniature coloured lamps or, better still, LEDs. Construction is shown in the diagrams in Fig 9/8 — when you come to think of it, it's fairly obvious, isn't it?

Above *A corner of Mike Sharman's fascinating period layout. Every model here is scratchbuilt, producing a highly distinctive layout at minimum outlay.*

Below *Ian Rice's 'Tregarrick', situated on the mythical North Cornwall Minerals Railway, recaptured the offbeat charm of the West Country industrial railway. Virtually everything on this model was scratchbuilt, since only Ian was interested enough to actually want such a model.*

Top *A corner of John Allison's 'Porth y Waen', an O gauge mineral branch in the diesel era. Both locomotives here, a Class '33' and a 'Hymek' are modified commercial products and quite inexpensive.*

Above *This small diesel shunter on John Allison's 'Porth y Waen' is an Continental import, dressed up as an industrial shunter and makes an inexpensive entry into O gauge modelling.*

Below *The turntable on Neville Hunt's 'Swaveny', a period layout built to P4 standards. Although of the highest quality, the fact that every model is scratchbuilt means the model is ideally suited for a tight budget.*

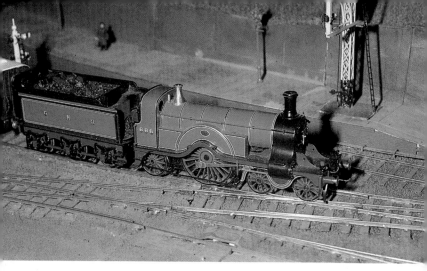

Above *This exquisite 4 mm scale Stirling single, built by Neville Hunt, is a fine example of what can be produced economically by careful scratchbuilding.*

Below *The entrance to 'Rewley Road', the Oxford MRC's model of the LMS (ex-LNWR) Oxford station. This sort of prototype model involves more in the way of study and effort than actual outlay. As drawings of many station buildings are now reasonably easy to locate in books and magazines, this makes an excellent project for the modeller on a limited budget.*

Above *Midport station on Ken Ashberry's 'Ashtown & Midport'. This compact type of station is ideally suited to the tight budget—it doesn't demand a lot of stock either!*

Below *An HST on the Crawley club's impressive diesel era layout. Because the locos and rolling stock in both OO and N gauges, are reasonably priced, the present day scene makes an excellent theme for the budget-conscious modeller.*

Bottom *Because Continental locos tend to be pricier than their British equivalents, a layout based on European practice needs careful budgeting. The end result can be well worthwhile, as this illustration shows.*

If you are using LEDs, you need a 3 v supply, or dropper resistors. Personally, I favour batteries, because then you're sure you're using only the 3 v that is required and since LEDs use very little current the question of battery life is not too significant. It is, of course, important to get the supply the right way round, for LED stands for Light Emitting Diode, and the wrong-way supply gives no light since the current is blocked by the diode. It's mainly a matter of trial and error, as by the time you've run the wires along the baseboard, you'll have forgotten which is which.

Semaphore signals can be made in the home workshop without too much difficulty. The arms, which appear to be the main problem are fairly easy to make on simple jigs. Fig 9/9 shows some methods. This is a job where batch construction pays dividends, since once you've worked out how to fabricate the particular arm you favour, work goes on swimmingly. A reasonable stock, built up one wet Saturday afternoon, will provide an ample number of arms for most layouts. It's an excellent idea to paint them in batches as well, for this is a tedious task when done one by one as there are at least three colours on the face and two on the rear, which means five distinct painting sessions, each separated by one day to allow the

Fig 9/9 *Semaphore arm construction.*

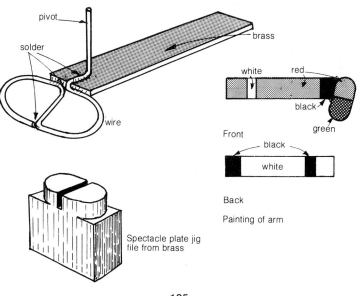

pivot

solder

brass

wire

white   red

black

green

Front

black

white

Back

Painting of arm

Spectacle plate jig
file from brass

105

paint to dry. Put that way, it's a week's work, but as each session would be only about an hour long, it's not too onerous, and at the end of the week, there's something tangible to show for your efforts.

Semaphore signal posts can be built from wood, but are very delicate, 4 mm square brass is much better. This is where home construction can score over commercial products, which are, today, either plastic or cast whitemetal.

Kits are available of course, ranging from the excellent Ratio range in plastic, to the very extensive 'Sprat & Winkle' range which provides superb replicas of most pre-group semaphore designs in 4 and 7 mm scales. If you can allow yourself one luxury, I would suggest top quality semaphore signals for, more than anything else, these very distinctive, railway-like features give real character to the model, whilst the fact that, as I said earlier, signals are something most people quietly forget, ensures that a well-signalled layout is automatically regarded as being of high quality.

The home signal, protecting the level crossing, is a vital part of this railway-like scene on Alan Wright's 'Cheviotdale'.

Fig 9/10 *Electrical operation of upper quadrant semaphore signal.*

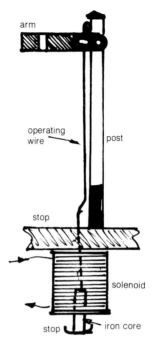

The mechanical system used for points may also be employed for semaphore signals, but here electrical systems are possible on a DIY basis. You need a supply of thin enamelled wire, plus a number of home-made bobbins, as shown in the diagram. These are tumble-wound with as much wire as you can get onto the bobbin, and then it's just a matter of arranging a simple steel armature onto the signal. Round nails are the favoured supply for the armatures. Fig 9/10 shows the basics of the system.

Signalling is a very extensive subject and has only recently been decently covered by books addressed to the amateur. If anyone wants to know how the full sized system sets about the job, then *British Railway Signalling* by Geoff Kichenside and Alan Williams provides ample accurate information, and has deservedly gone into several editions. There are also more costly, but very exhaustive studies of the detailed practice of individual railway companies if you get thoroughly hooked on the subject.

Signals are important. If there is one single feature that distinguishes a serious model railway from an overgrown train set it is that the former has signals, and the drivers obey them.

POWER SUPPLIES

The message of this chapter is simple, there are very few ways you can materially reduce the basic cost of power supplies and electrification in general. Worse, they all depend on two factors, the first, a very detailed knowledge of the subject based on long experience and a large slice of luck. There are, however, various routes that *appear* to cut costs, but which merely increase them, such as the aquisition of an unsuitable power unit.

If you are going to operate a model railway, as opposed to merely play trains in an aimless fashion, then your initial power unit should supply 12 v dc, at a maximum 1.5 a output; an independent 16 v ac at a nominal 20 va rating; and a controller which allows the dc output to be reversed in polarity and modified in voltage to permit both the direction and speed of the model to be controlled as you wish. These are the rock-bottom basic requirements, and although you can get by, after a fashion, with less, the development of the model will be severely hampered.

In addition, the unit should contain internal protection against overload, and be constructed to meet the not unduly onerous safety levels laid down in regulations. Omission of the first can lead to an accidental wrecking of the unit, failure to observe the second could, under unfavourable conditions, be lethal. Moreover, the fact that some very old equipment may not meet current safety standards makes the purchase of second-hand equipment something of a gamble. It is as well to play safe and buy a guaranteed unit from a reputable manufacturer.

It is also essential to be scrupulously careful over the connection to the ac mains supply. For a start, the lead from the unit rarely reaches to the power socket. What you must *never* do is to extend the lead by hooking any odd length of flex to it by means of a 'twiddle' joint wrapped in 'insulating' tape, this is extremely dangerous. The simplest solution is to invest in a short extension lead with a four-way socket, and plug this into the mains socket, and use it for not only the power units, but also for the soldering iron electric drill and so on. If you want to add an electric heater, then the lead should be of 13 a capacity, otherwise 3 a is adequate. If you need a local heater, then use a fan heater, the low-level radiant around a layout, is potentially dangerous from every angle. Above all, unless you do know what to do, leave all aspects of mains electricity to qualified professionals.

One tempting way of running an initial project is a bargain

A *small control panel incorporating an ECM electronic controller module and a selection of miniature switches.*

controller bought at an exhibition. Watch out! There are a number of elementary 'controllers' produced for train set use which have an extremely low output and the crudest of controls — often, in effect, three speeds, very fast, fast and stop! If you happen to have such a unit already, all well and good, but don't waste your money buying one. On the other hand there are some very simple units which offer just a 12 v controlled output at around 10 va rating — in practice, a nominal output of nearly 1 a. They will run a single locomotive, but won't do anything else — operate points, provide a lighting circuit and so on. However, as one usually ends up by wanting to have two controllers, such a unit can make an excellent first choice if it is absolutely essential to begin at the lowest possible cost. You just accept that you can't afford remote control of points, or the luxury of lighting for the time being.

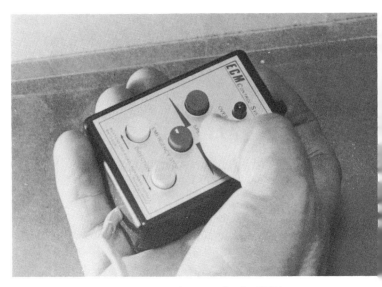

An advanced hand-held electronic controller by ECM.

There are some extremely elaborate controllers about, with masses of special features. In particular, the command control systems, such as the Hornby Zero 1 appear to have advantages. In my opinion, the value of this system, on a serious model railway is open to question. In addition its correct implementation is extremely expensive. In my opinion (which is not necessarily correct!) if you want to play with a computer, buy a computer, but don't use it to run your layout.

The electronic controller, usually produced as a module for building into your own control panel, but also available as a hand-held unit, is a different matter, and unless the budget is very tight, is well worth considering. Most operate off a 16 v ac supply, and can be operated from the auxiliary output of a standard power unit and so can always be added to the layout at a later stage.

However, the hand-held controller allows the operator to move around the model and, since this gives him the best view of the trains — which is extremely desirable — it is an option that many modellers take either at the outset, or early in the development of the model. A distinct advantage is that, in freeing the operator from a fixed position, there is no need to provide centralized control of turnouts — which is a great saving.

You will come across cases where enthusiasts have built their own power supplies. The reason for this is that the user requires a non-standard specification. This is so in my own case, I want things like 6.3 v ac for lighting, smoothed 24 v dc for relays, plus a couple of other odds and ends for which, not surprisingly, there is insufficient demand to warrant production. I also have, and use, several perfectly standard control units which I find are more convenient during the build-up stages. Constructing your own power supply is not really cost effective.

Building your own controller is also not particularly cheap. Way back in the '40s and early '50s, in the heyday of the ex-government surplus store, one could get hold of some useful bits and pieces. In those days, if you had a good hunt around the back streets of Soho you could track down things like the lovely Ohmite 100 ohm variable wirewound resistors, which, coupled with a DPDT toggle switch, made a very good controller for around 5/-. In fact, those Ohmite resistors were so beautifully made they are still working to this day — which is hardly surprising when you look at the current catalogue price and study the manufacturer's specification. Indeed, one reason why electronic controllers are growing in favour is that they are cheaper to build. If you've a mind that way, there are some excellent books on the subject of electronics such as *Practical*

A home-made panel incorporating resistance control. The main controller is an ex-government 100 ohm 'Ohmite' wirewound resistance, now, alas, only obtainable at a high price.

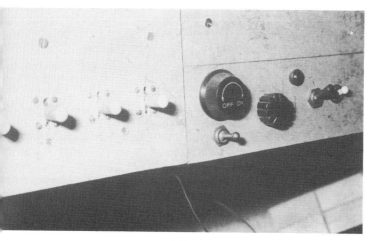

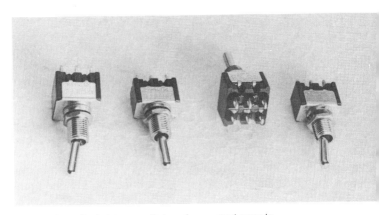

A selection of miniature switches for control panels.

Electronics for Railway Modellers Vols 1 and 2, by Roger Amos (PSL) but, because electronic components come very much cheaper if you can buy in 100+ lots, you can usually get a commercial unit, properly constructed, thoroughly guaranteed, for little more than the cost, to you, of the necessary bits and pieces

You will in any case need a number of switches and a large quantity of wire. If you shop around, you can make some saving here. Proops of Tottenham Court Road have a good range of new toggle switches at competitive prices, and, doubtless, other suppliers can be found in the provinces. It is occasionally possible to get suitable wire in bargain lots, and, as you need a large quantity it makes good sense to buy in 100 m coils. Unless you have money to burn, don't bother with colour coding, this can only be effective you can afford to stock at least a kilometer of wire in total so that whatever your requirements might be, you never run out of specific colour. Needless to say, you end up with a lot of the colour you rarely use. What happens, in 99 cases out of a hundred, is that you run out of red wire, but still have ample green — at that point you realize that colour coding is rather pointless.

It's often possible to obtain scrap multi-core cable, cheap. If it is ex-British Telecom, then except for short runs, you need to double up on the wire, as there is a very significant different between the current flow in telephone and model railway circuits. Other than this, the two systems are remarkably alike, with the result that, to the knowledgeable, ex-GPO, or ex-Telecom equipment is extreme useful. As it is made to very high standards, the ex-equipment

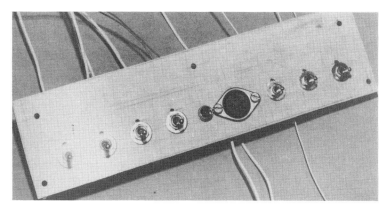

A simple panel using miniature switches. The socket is for a hand-held electronic controller.

throwouts are generally in first class order. Unfortunately, this only applies to the old relay based technology, the modern System X is solid state, and won't work at our current levels.

In conclusion, the best way to keep an electrical control system down to a tight budget is to avoid all frills. In particular, to save money, don't go in for the 'Mighty Wurlitzer' pattern control panel, for they are a pure luxury. On the other hand, they are great fun!

DIRT CHEAP SCENERY

On all but the simplest of model railways, some attempt is made to model the immediate surroundings of the line. With one glorious exception, the urban line, usually hemmed in with retaining walls or more occasionally, modelled along the top of a viaduct, this involves some landscaping, and with it the reproduction of the ground surface. There are any number of ways of setting about this, and, of course, you will discover that a number of firms are happy to sell you various concoctions. They often have on display some very beautiful models, and, if you meet them at an exhibition they will convince you that their methods — and materials — give the best results. Until, that is, you meet the next scenic expert who will spin you exactly the same yarn, but will push his pet system, which is, naturally, totally different. Don't panic — they *all* work. The truth is that when modelling a landscape the materials and methods are not critical, t'ain't what you do, it's the way that you do it!

The exact form of the ground surface depends on the underlying strata but, within the confines of a normal model railway, this is not very critical as you're only modelling a very tiny sample of the whole. As usual, you study the prototype, and if it happens to be a fair way off, you use a good picture book. If the scenery is worth modelling, *someone* will have published a colourful pictorial guide book.

What we have to do is to produce an undulating surface that looks reasonably natural. This is remarkably easy, and the methods I propose to describe (which are by no means the only ones) happen to be fairly flexible during construction. The first system is also very cheap since the main material is one which, in the average household is not only thrown away, but usually takes up far too much space in the dustbin — old newspapers.

Newsprint is a cheap, open-weave paper, and is very absorbent. If you paste around six to eight layers on top of each other, alllowing time to dry in between, you end up with a thin shell that is a very rough form of cardboard. So all you need apart from old newspapers is paste. The most suitable, the cheapest and most easily available is wallpaper adhesive.

Clearly, you don't want to mix up a bucket full, as the instructions suggest, so you also need a screw top jar to keep the surplus wallpaper paste powder in. You also need something to mix the paste in, again a screw-top glass jar is useful, and a cheap brush, about 20 to 25 mm wide. The only other essential is a piece of scrap board about 300 mm by 150 mm on which to paste the bits of paper.

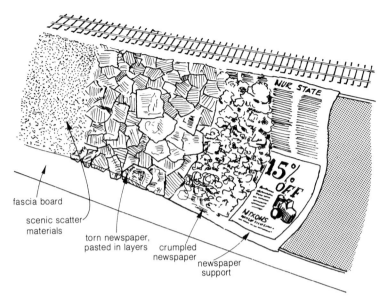

fascia board

scenic scatter materials

torn newspaper, pasted in layers

crumpled newspaper

newspaper support

Fig 11/1 *Stages in constructing model landscape from pasted newspapers.*

There are other optional blobs and dabs you can use if you're so minded, but these are the essentials.

The process is shown, diagramatically, in Fig 11/1. We begin by preparing a sub-base for the landscape. This is made from more newspaper. The first step is to cover the gap with a single sheet, which can at this stage, sag a fair amount. It can be pasted down, stuck with sticky tape, or even pinned. You now dampen it slightly to make it cling to the edge of your framework.

Now form the surface you intend to model with crumpled newspaper. It's best to tear each sheet into pieces around 200 mm square (don't take this too literally) and to make fairly small balls, which you hold in place with dabs of paste. Wallpaper paste does hold things fairly firmly even when wet, otherwise you'd never be able to paper a wall, let alone a ceiling. It also has 'slip' so you can jiggle parts about for a good long while until you get them more or less as you want them.

Once the shape of your crumpled paper is about right, you start pasting the top layer. Initially, you need fairly big bits of paper, which are laid loosely over the foundation, but once the first layer is in

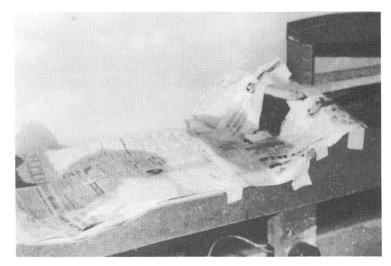

Above *Landscape construction using a newspaper base. This shows the main area with the initial layer in place, further layers are pasted over this foundation.*

Below *An effective section of landscape construction.*

place, you can use smaller sections. Furthermore, as you proceed, you can begin to mould the slippery top layer of pasted paper into an even closer approximation of your desired ground surface. Use the brush, not your fingers.

You will be able to paste three to four layers before the ground surface begins to get too soggy for safety. After washing out the brush, cleaning out the paste jar and picking up all the surplus newspaper, wash your hands and proceed to some other task whilst leaving the scenery to harden.

While we're waiting for the initial coating to dry, there are a couple of points to mention. If you are doing this in the garage, or a separate railway room, fine — you don't have to worry. If you're doing it inside the house, then it's certain you're doing it over a carpet and as carpets are not improved with a coating of wallpaper paste, do lay something down beforehand. More newspaper is adequate, and can be rolled into a large ball at the conclusion of one evening's activities, but a sizeable length of plastic sheet is even better, providing it has no holes.

When the first coating is good and dry, you can go on to the next. providing nothing of the initial paste-up is above the proposed ground level, you've no worries, if you have an unwanted hump, you have the slight bother of cutting it away and filling in the hole to the correct level. Fortunately, this isn't too difficult once the initial pasted paper has properly hardened, a good sharp modelling knife will cut through three or four layers of pasted newsprint with minimal difficulty. Indeed, one of the great virtues of this type of landscape cover is that it is relatively easy to carve holes in it, using a stiff sharp knife. Why should you want to carve holes in your painstakingly modelled landscape? Simple, to accommodate the bright idea you get soon after the landscape is finished. Again, don't panic, just remember civil engineering projects and building construction begin with a hole in the ground.

To digress a little, on an open top section, you will find that anything from 40 to 80 per cent of the baseboard area is now made from old newspaper, plus a little paste and, of course, your time. Leaving aside any question of the improvement in appearance brought about by some nicely rendered rolling landscape, the sheer saving in cost is considerable. For this reason alone, it makes good sense, on anything but the most compact of layouts, to incorporate a fair amount of landscape into the model. Indeed, because landscaping is so cheap, you can, on larger schemes, cover the proposed site for a later station or other railway feature with a pleasing piece of countryside. In other words, just as on the prototype, you have the landscape before you build the station.

To get back to our landscape, we've now got the main outline in place, but with only four thickness of pasted newsprint, it's very flimsy. You now proceed much as before, laying down four or five coats of paper. Once again, you leave it to dry. The number of layers you apply depends to a large extent on how long you are prepared to continue, for clearly, the thicker the layer, within reason, the better. The only snag is the time it takes to dry between coats. The thicker the underlying base the more coats you can apply before the base becomes soggy though, by the same token, the longer it takes to harden again.

Once you've produced a fairly firm foundation, and the final coating is dry, the supporting newsprint can be torn away and disposed of. I'm assuming that you've been modelling over an open baseboard, but if you're producing a piece of scenery over a solid section, then you just leave the paper support in place. It won't do any harm.

A slightly more expensive but faster process is to replace wallpaper paste with plaster. Here the process differs slightly. First you need a small bowl in which to mix the plaster. The most convenient is the plastic container that is used for ice-cream, a fairly flexible box with nice rounded corners. The reason for the flexible plastic is that when the plaster hardens — which it will, inexorably — you simply turn the container upside down and bend it about until the lumps fall off — onto a sheet of newspaper, please!

Although any plaster can be used, the proprietary crack filler (such as Polyfilla) is not ideal — it's too slow to set. The best is a hard casting compound, here Boots dental plaster is probably the most convenient. Normal builders' plaster (Kean's cement) is quite good.

Prepare the base with crumpled newspaper as before, then tear up small bits of newspaper. Mix the plaster to a creamy consistency, about that of the batter used in fish-shops, then take the pieces of newspaper and coat them in the plaster. The correct technique is that used by fish fryers, so wander down to your local chippie and study form whilst waiting for your cod 'n chips! Slap the plastered newsprint in place and leave it to dry. With most plasters, this will take between five and fifteen minutes. As a result, this system is fairly quick.

Plaster scenic construction is great fun, even better than mud pies but it is also *extremely* messy. So, cover the carpet. Plaster *will*

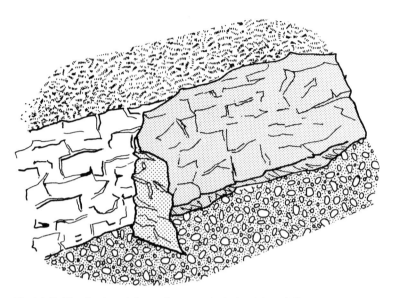

Fig 11/2 'Casting' rock faces in crumpled aluminium foil.

brush out of carpets, but I know of no way of convincing a spouse that this works. A practical demonstration is turned aside with the comment 'you were lucky that time'. On the whole, even if your living room carpet is guaranteed by the manufacturer to be resistant to every form of stain known to mankind, it is best not to get anything on it in the first instance. Apart from anything else, you don't want to be in the invidious position of proving the manufacturer wrong, because he (if a corporation can have a gender) will be even more difficult to convince than your other half. It is also a good idea to wear old clothes and to have a bucket of warm water handy in which to wash your hands. (It can be cold if you're a stoic). An old but serviceable towel is also needed to dry them with afterwards.

Rock faces need to be made from plaster. There are various methods which have been used with considerable success, but the one I prefer happens to be very simple. You take a piece of kitchen foil and crumple it. You plaster over your rock face and slap the crumpled kitchen foil over it. When dry, peel off the foil. In Fig 11/2 I show the general idea. It's surprisingly realistic. You can leave things as they are, or you can do a little judicious carving to improve matters. You can paint plaster with any paint you fancy, I prefer

Plaster rockfaces surrounded this 3.5 mm scale scene.

water-based paints which are quickly absorbed into the plaster. But I digress, not everyone needs a rock face on their layout.

If we go back to the pasted paper or plaster shell, you have a nice undulating surface which mainly cost you little more than a number of evenings' work. It is however, anything but the correct colour. Well, the plaster might just pass on a darkish night for a scoured section of the South Downs, but newsprint — never! It needs texturing.

There are numerous proprietary scatter materials on the market. Many, if you inspect them closely, are fundamentally sawdust, which is fairly easy to obtain from your local timber yard, though I get all I need during baseboard construction, and furthermore, the sawdust produced by a home sawbench is finer, and thus more suitable, than the stuff hacked out by the larger, coarser blade on the professional sawbench. Once you have your sawdust you can dye it, or you can soak it in well diluted model paint. This can be

A well-developed corner of an O gauge layout, with some effective contrasts in scenic construction. The cut-out flats in front of the backscene proper appear a little obtrusive in this picture, but this is due to the fact that the camera was held over the baseboard at an unusual angle that would not be adopted by this normal viewer.

done in yet another screw-top glass jar. You then need to spread it out to dry.

What you need here are a selection of flat trays of varying sizes. If you keep a good look out, you'll probably find plenty lying about the place. They need to be safely mounted above a radiator, or placed inside the oven after cooking — though I don't personally like that idea. Never use the oven if you're using a plastic tray, the resulting mess beggars description and is, I understand, extremely unpopular with the cook.

Naturally, you mix up various shades of green, plus a few other hues, yellow, blue and several browns are the most useful. Nature does not employ a uniform colour scheme. More screw-top jars are needed to store the various colours, so begin collecting them whilst you are in the planning stages of the model.

There are other useful texturing materials. Used tealeaves, once dried, make excellent foliage. Coffee grounds have been used for ballast and also for rough gravel or dirt. Fine sand is also very handy. Once again, the ubiquituous screw-top jar comes into its own, I did say you'd need all you could get.

Scenic textures are generally stuck down with PVA adhesive, but another method is to use old oil-based paint. You want a green or brown colour, and although you can go out and buy the stuff, it is often the case that you have the tag-end of gloss paint and undercoat left over from the last bout of home decoration.

Trees can be built up on a wire frame. The fine copper wire found in old telephone cables is quite good for this, but any softish wire will do. The idea is to make a wire replica of a tree-trunk with its branches and then, when correctly shaped, the foliage is added, using any suitable material — dried tea leaves are excellent, the only problem is remembering not to throw them away in the first place.

There are two general approaches. One is to take a long time lovingly reproducing an actual tree. This is the best approach where very few trees are needed, but demands a certain amount of patience and perseverance, not to mention careful study of the real thing. There are several inexpensive colour books which show British trees in summer and winter guise, these show the character-istic structure of the branches and the way the foliage is clumped and are much more convenient than going out to look at the full-sized original. Though I must admit, I like to look at trees for their own sake.

The other method, which is best if you intend to have fairly large numbers of trees, is to produce a quantity of wire frames as quickly as you can, make up the trees in an equal hurry and then sort them into three categories, the reasonably realistic ones that you put in the front, with choice specimens given a *solus* location, the second grade which can form small copses, and the rather indifferent 'wood' trees that are placed, *en masse*, behind the second grade to form woods.

Scouring pads help form the foliage, and although they cost something, the cheaper sort — those you find in street markets — are better for this purpose than the branded types, which generally have a very strong, firm structure with the idea of lasting longer. The point is, we don't want 'em to last, we want to tease them into a

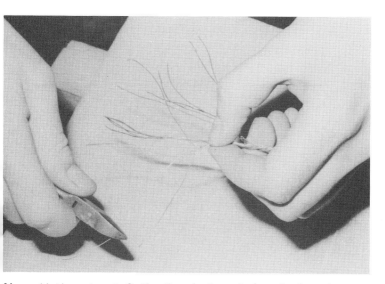

Above *Making a tree 1: Cutting the wire loops to form the branches.*

Below *Making a tree 2: Forming the shape of the tree.*

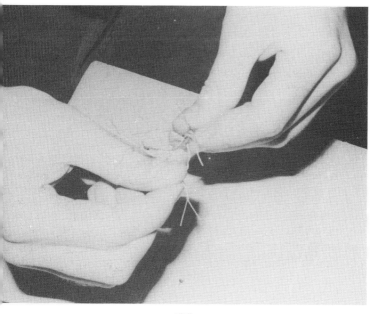

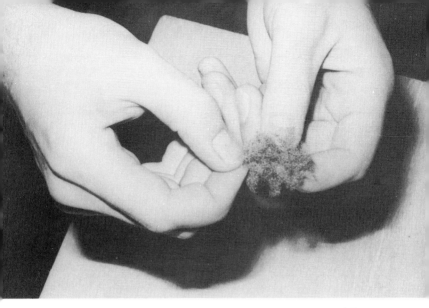

Above *Making a tree 3: Teasing the scouring pads into foliage.*

Below *Making a tree 4: Applying glue to the wire branches. Note that these have been painted heavily to hide the wire.*

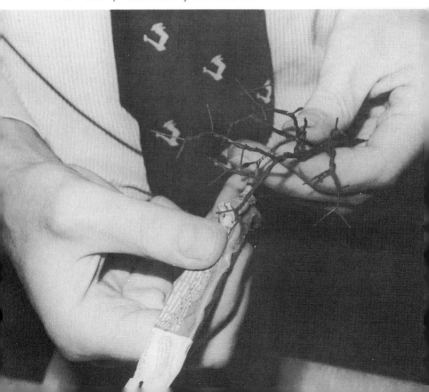

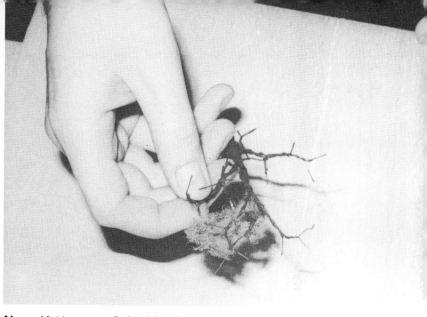

Above *Making a tree 5: Applying the teased out scouring pad to the tree.*

Below *Making a tree 6: The completed tree.*

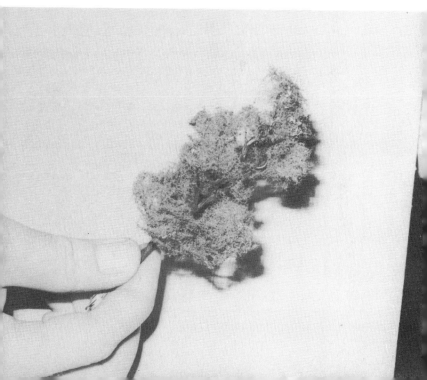

Above *a good example of a wire-based tree on Martin Brent's 'Rye Harbour'. The foliage here is a high quality commercial brand by Woodland Scenics.*

Below Fig 11/3 *Simple tree construction.*

Key: **1** *Loops of thin copper wire twisted at one end. The other end is cut as indicated.* **2** *The cut ends are teased out. The 'trunk' can be coated with epoxy resin and left to harden overnight.* **3** *Foliage is added to the wires, using teased scouring pads as a foundation. Finally the tree is painted.*

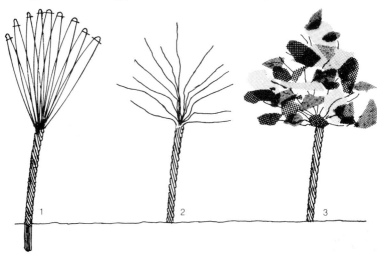

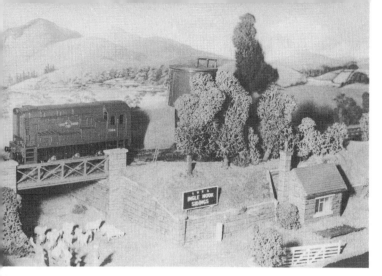

A bank of trees on Alan Wright's 'Inglenook Sidings': each tree is made from dyed lichen on a twig foundation. This is very simple and quick, but not quite as realistic as the wire and scouring pad method.

oose, open form. Again, they're dressed with foliage materials. One material you should shun is wire wool, which has, on many occasions been recommended for this purpose. The trouble is that t is easily picked up by the powerful permanent magnets fitted to your locomotives and it does the mechanisms no good whatever.

Fig 11/3 shows the basis principles, and although this does appear extremly simple and a trifle haphazard, it is the method used by the MRC 2 mm scale group to produce trees for their prize-winning 'Chiltern Green' layout. Photographs of tree making in progress at the MRC are also included. Hedges can also be teased out of scouring pads. If you can come across some rubberized horsehair, as used in top quality upholstery, so much the better. Both foundations need some foliage added to taste. You can also get dyed lichen in model shops, this, sparingly used, produces further types of ground cover and can also be used for making trees.

Modelling gardens and allotments, not to mention fields of corn, or other crops, calls for more advanced techniques. You don't have to go so far as they do at Pendon Museum, where modellers have been known to build up hollyhocks, petal by petal and leaf by leaf, but you do need to do a good deal of specialized work. Probably the best way is to find someone who's done it already and ask. This is best done at exhibitions, there are few modellers who aren't both flattered by such a request and anxious to pass on their knowledge. It's that sort of hobby.

BRIDGES, VIADUCTS AND TUNNELS

Bridges, viaducts, tunnel portals and other civil engineering structures form a distinctive part of any railway, prototype or model, as more than anything else, they are the symbol of the railway age. They are made, in the main, from three principal materials, brick, stone and iron. I say iron rather than steel, since quite a few early bridges were made from cast iron, whilst many others were built from wrought iron before Bessemer and his successors made steel readily available.

Brick was the commonest material of the railway age, in particular the distinctive hard blue engineering brick, favoured through the latter half of the nineteenth century. Victorian brickwork is extremely fine, it is also remarkably strong, as quite a few demolition contractors have since discovered. Railway brickwork was made to last! As a result, even despite the ravages of

Masonry overbridge on Alan Wright's 'Cheviotdale' 4 mm scale layout. The stonework is represented by embossed styrene sheet, appropriately painted.

modernization and the relentless march of the developer's bull-dozer, our cities and towns possess many good examples of Victorian structures where the intricate nature of the then fashionable decorative brickwork may be studied by the interested modelmaker.

Stone, generally but not exclusively in the form of squared masonry was also greatly favoured by railway engineers. One can assume that when a line had to carve through rock strata, a good deal of useable structural stone became available.

Ironwork varied from the simple plate girder to the intricacies of a cantilever bridge. Agreed, few modellers are likely to be able to model the latter prototype, but there are ample patterns for simpler trussed girder spans for the ambitious modeller to copy.

Cast iron, though used extensively in the first half of the nineteenth century, is today, rare for underbridges, and none too common on overbridges either, but the grace of this class of structure makes it worthy of inclusion somewhere around the layout. Whilst dealing with earlier bridging materials one must not forget timber. Although the majority of timber bridges disappeared before World War 2, it was a popular material with the early engineers, and, if anything, even more popular with those model-makers who have discovered that an apparently complex structure is relatively easy to model by aping prototype procedure, thus, in one stroke, not only acquiring a distinctive model, but also gaining the respect of those of their friends who haven't, as yet, read this book.

Which brings me to the nub of the argument. Although kits exist, and are not unduly expensive, this is an area where the individual model, produced to fit the site, pays exceptional dividends simply because prototypes are so infinitely varied that the modeller has little difficulty in finding something which is both absolutely right for his chosen area and prototype and also quite unique to his own layout.

Clearly, one needs to begin with something simple and fairly straightforward, here I suggest that the masonry bridge is a good starting point. Fig 12/1 shows the basic principles, the sides being cut from ply — generally 3 to 4 mm in thickness — with a road surface from hardboard or thin ply. A lot depends on the contents of one's timber stock.

The two sides need to be more or less identical and this is easily arranged by cutting them out together. I've always preferred to pin the two sheets together in the waste areas, then cut away with a

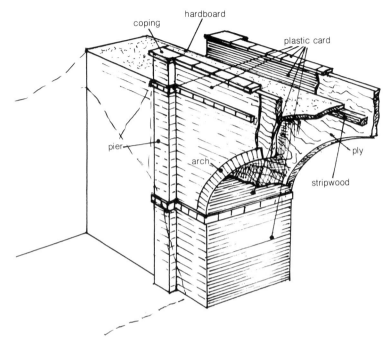

Fig 12/1 *Construction of a model masonry arch bridge.*

fretsaw so that, finally, the two halves fall apart. The road-bed is fixed by pinning and glueing to stripwood bearers.

Stripwood is a basic modelmaker's material, which can be bought from any model shop worthy of the name. However, it's surprising how much effective stripwood is produced more or less by accident as one cuts up timber for other projects. Of course, where stripwood is required as a structural material in its own right, it is important that it is made to scale sizes, but where, as is so often the case, it is only required as a reinforcing member or as a support, the precise size is irrelevant. So, keep offcuts of wood, it's surprising how often you need them. Once the sides and road-bed are fixed together, the overall shape of the bridge begins to take form. Some cross-bracing may be needed internally but more offcuts of timber can be used for this.

The completed carcass requires surfacing. In the diagram I have suggested plastic sheet surfaces, with the idea of using one of the many embossed versions to give the texture which adds something extra to the finish of the model. However, brickpaper may be used instead — this is a matter of personal choice — but there is an alternative which has one great virtue, it is cheap!

If you take a sheet of thin, easily-cut material such as card and ideally something that cost next to nothing to begin with, and paint it roughly in either stone or brick colour, then cut it into brick or stone-sized pieces, you end up with a large supply of model wall surfacing. Spread a small area of the model with adhesive — generally PVA latex — and pick up the surface stone by stone and put it in place on the model, bonding as you go along. It sounds incredibly tedious, but in practice, it is nowhere near so tricky as it appears. Cutting the sheet into small pieces in the first instance is probably the most tedious part of the whole affair! In the past many modellers have made use of computer chads, the tiny rectangles churned out when punched cards are produced. The only snag with this is that no-one, so far as I know, uses anything but magnetic media for computer data storage today and whilst I did hear of one group who were supposed to have obtained a card puncher from a former user at a

This superb masonry viaduct is an exact 2 mm scale model of one on the former Midland main line near Chiltern Green, and formed a prominent part of the Model Railway Club's prizewinning 'Chiltern Green' layout.

The late Jack Nelson built this section of Runcorn Bridge in 3.5 mm scale as part of an ambitious diorama layout featuring several sections of the LNWR in the Liverpool area.

give-away price, I've yet to see any products from it. It's probably one of those myths.

The 'laying' of model bricks or stone blocks calls for a small amount of patience, and a sharp pointed instrument with which to pick up the individual blocks. You can do it with the point of a scalpel, or craft knife. Some people advise a needle held in a piece of wood, whilst there are some similar tools, designed for cutting screen dot overlays in graphical design, which are very effective. However, the probability is that you have the scalpel or craft knife to hand whilst you're modelling.

It is, I think, best to begin with the vital parts, the arch and the quoins (if any), then apply the main courses. The raised string courses are easily applied over the base courses. Clearly, you should begin with a fairly simple system and only move on to the more elaborate arrangements as you master the technique. Whilst on the subject, when working with brickpaper, the arches and quoins are generally applied over the base covering, the slight difference in thickness is virtually unnoticeable. String courses are made by pasting strips of brickpaper onto thin card, then slitting the card when dry into narrow strips. Where embossed plastic sheet is used, it is essential to cut the base sheet to take the arch, if the surface is to be flush. Fortunately, projecting quoins are quite common, so if these are individually cut from 10 thou plastic sheet, you can apply them over the base.

Before I move on to other forms of bridge, I must briefly mention the tunnel mouth, which is, in practice, half a masonry arch. Fig 12/2 shows the general construction, and depicts one of the more elaborate facades. For some reason, the early engineers were at pains to produce elaborate tunnel portals, but as, in general, they were set in locations where few could see them, the purpose remains obscure. A drawing of one of these appears as Fig 12/3. This is an interesting elevation, for the historic drawing from which I worked gave the location as Linslade on the original London & Birmingham. There is just one niggling detail, the prototype tunnel looks nothing like this! There are three categories of falsehood, lies, damned lies and general arrangement drawings!

Fig 12/2 *Construction of a model tunnel mouth.*

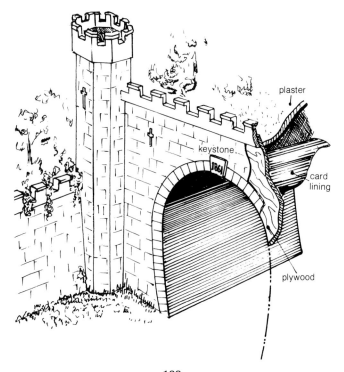

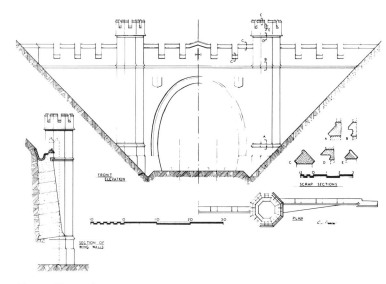

FRONT
ELEVATION

SCRAP SECTIONS

PLAN

SECTION OF
WING WALLS

Above Fig 12/3 *Elevation of 'Linslade Tunnel', London & Birmingham Railway.*

Below *This ornate tunnel mouth on 'Cheviotdale' comes from a Faller plastic kit and is a copy of the facades on one of the lines through the Loreley rock on the Rhine. It's not out of keeping with a British scene, and as an impressive structure, is probably well worth the cost to anyone with a reasonable budget.*

A low viaduct on Alan Wright's 'Cheviotdale' layout. The girders are made from bits of plastic kits around a plywood deck—which actually provides most of the strength!

Model tunnels, unlike the prototype, are clearly visible to viewers, so the extra work needed to produce a castellated version is well worthwhile. E. W. Twining provided a number of excellent drawings in early volumes of *Model Engineer* but as few will have access to these magazines, it's fortunate that smaller reproductions appeared in his book *Indoor Model Railways* which, whilst out of print these many years, is a little more accessible.

Girder bridges fall into two main categories, the straightforward plate girder and the more elaborate truss. A good model of a braced truss is a thing of beauty, but it also involves a great deal of work, and does required a fair knowledge of the prototype. Hence, it is strictly an advanced project for the individual, or more likely, one of those cases where the kit saves a good deal of effort and is accordingly, cost effective. However, in practice, braced girders are only used for the longer spans, and for the majority of models, plate girders are quite acceptable.

Once again, it does help to study the prototype, even though the design is more or less standardized. Fig 12/4 shows a fairly normal plate girder, note in particular the way the top and bottom flange is made up from several thicknesses of sheet, producing a thicker

135

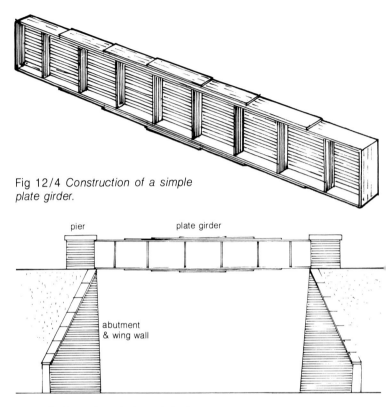

Fig 12/4 *Construction of a simple plate girder.*

pier

plate girder

abutment & wing wall

Fig 12/5 *Elevation of plate girder bridge, showing abutments.*

section in the centre of the span, where the stresses are highest.

As the prototype is not produced from a single sheet of iron or, in later days, steel, there are lap joints to contend with, and angle irons are employed to support the various flanges. Whilst good quality card used to be favoured, this is an area where I, for one, believe that plastic card is the ideal material to use. A useful point to remember is the old rule of thumb formula for the proportions: 'the depth of the girder in inches is half the span in feet' — a ratio of 24:1 in other words. Whilst I doubt if any sizeable girder was designed in that haphazard fashion, the formula works superbly on a model, where the bridge itself is usually supported by the deck.

A girder bridge rests on abutments and piers as shown in Fig

12/5. Well, to be exact, all bridges have abutments and piers but it's a technical point on the masonry pattern where the arch stops and the abutment begins. Abutments are solid structures which generally have some form of wing wall to keep back loose earth. Once again, a careful study of the prototype will be very useful.

Mass concrete bridges, commonplace on motorways, are rare on railways as most of the lines were built before the material came into general use. However, as concrete structures are fairly easy to model — they are simply cut from wood — it is worth considering adding one or two, providing the period of the layout is post-1930. I am, of course, excluding a model of the West Highland, which used concrete extensively long before this date. The main thing to bear in mind when modelling concrete is to make it look like concrete. As a result, it is absolutely essential to fill the grain of any wood used, and then to paint it with care.

I turn now to the oldest bridging material, timber. There are few timber bridges left under or over a railway, but there were enough around in the early '30s to allow modellers to consider this material.

Brunel's graceful fan viaducts are a popular subject for modellers as they look far more complicated than they actually are. This is probably the best known of all such models, the 4 mm scale replica of Walkham Viaduct in the Pendon Museum. This is a very early picture taken when the model was still quite new and was housed in an old Army hut. The present museum was actually built around the model.

A detail of the Pendon Walkham Viaduct model showing one of the fans from underneath.

For once, the prototype material is best, though clearly, one uses a fairly fine grained timber.

The favoured material is balsa or obechi strip, sold mainly in model shops catering for aircraft modelling. If you have access to a small sawbench and have a supply of straight grained hardwood scrap to hand, then it is feasible to produce your own. The Unimat sawbench attachment, which fits on the tool-rest of the lathe, is ideal for this purpose, as the cut can be adjusted to very fine limits — in the order of 0.01 mm — but clearly, this is not exactly a cost-effective solution, as you can buy enough stripwood for most modelling purposes for the cost of the sawbench attachment alone, let alone the price of the Unimat!

Any timber structure consists of numerous struts, piers, beams and so on, which are all, without exception, cut to fairly precise lengths. If you set about cutting each of the many parts individually, you will not only go steadily crazy, but you will, in addition, end up with a lot of pieces which are *almost* identical in size.

To get round both these difficulties, you take a number of lengths of stripwood and make them into a large square section block usually made from eight, nine or twelve lengths, as in Fig 12/6. The block is held together by strips of Sellotape, and then is cut into precise lengths. Here, I feel investment in an Xacto mitre block is well worthwhile. It is a precision instrument, made from an extruded aluminium section, and gives square and 45° cuts without bother. The slots are, I find, able to take a standard 6 in pin-ended sawblade as well as the razor saws for which the tool is intended.

Assembly of a timber bridge calls for a little pre-planning. The various frames, are marked out full size on paper and the paper is then fixed down to a suitable base — Sundeala semi-hardboard is ideal. The next process I advise is covering the whole with a tightly

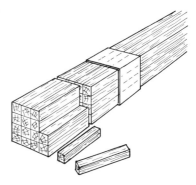

Below Fig 12/7 *Jig for assembling sections of timber trestle.*

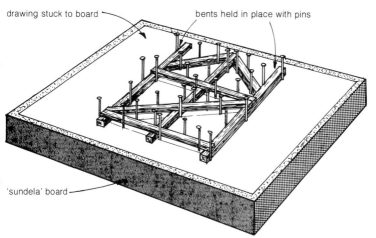

drawing stuck to board

bents held in place with pins

'sundela' board

drawn sheet of completely clear polythene, so that nothing will stick to the surface. Now, the various bents (the lengths of timbers) are placed over the drawing and glued together. Old fashioned acetate-based cements are still as good for this as they were in the early days of aircraft modelling, where this technique originated. The bents are held in place with pins whilst setting, these are placed on either side as shown in Fig 12/7. Where several identical frames are required, you simply leave the majority of the pins in place for the second frame. I stress 'majority' as I've never found it possible to prise the first frame out with all the pins left in the board, but as it's quite easy to put them back into their holes, it's a straightforward business of removing just sufficient to free the structure.

Although this sounds a lot of bother, it is quite simple to do in

139

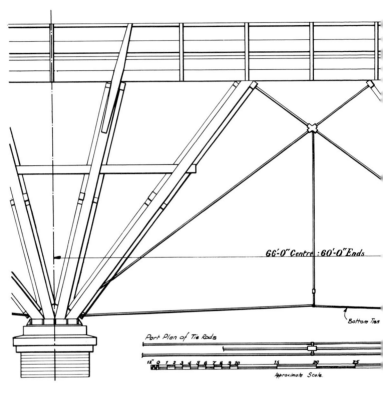

66'-0" Centre : 60'-0" Ends

Bottom Ties

Part Plan of Tie Rods

15   0 1 2 3 4 5 6 7 8 9 10   15   20   25

Approximate Scale.

GREAT   WESTERN

140

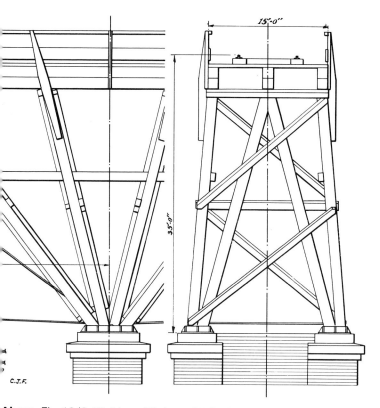

15'-0"

3'-5'-0"

C.J.F.

Above Fig 12/8 *Walkham Viaduct, GWR Tavistock Branch. The most advanced of the many Brunel fan viaducts.*

Left *You don't need an enormous space for a timber viaduct, this model has just two spans and, although part of a 4 mm scale layout, is actually built to ⅛ in-to-the-foot scale. This is a useful way of fitting a large civil engineering structure into a small model—few people are aware of the true size of viaduct, and with the proportions maintained, the eye is deceived.*

practice. Oddly enough, one of the easiest timber structures to attempt at the outset is the Brunel timber fan, which is made from four (occasionally, three) frames per pier, which, as there are only two frame designs involved, makes the structure amenable to rapid construction. Fig 12/8 provides the main details of construction, together with the leading dimensions. This drawing shows Walkham Viaduct, the most elegant of the fans, for full details I recommend a

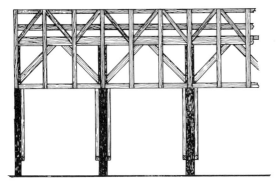

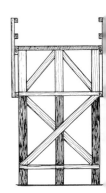

Above Fig 12/9 *A timber trestle bridge.*

Left Fig 12/10 *Sketch of a brick retaining wall.*

study of Dick Woodfin's *History of the Cornwall Railway.* This book contains thumbnail sketches of all the Cornish viaducts and as the leading dimensions were identical, you can go on from there. Fig 12/9 gives further details for the simple piled construction found in piers and jetties which, again make excellent subjects for model-making. Certainly, timber bridges, if remotely appropriate to your chosen scene, are well worth adding to the model.

To weather the timber, almost any thin colouring material may be used. Diluted Indian ink, wood dye, oil paint well let down with thinners have all been used with success. One thing you shouldn't use is creosote. It is, of course, the correct colour, but the pungent smell takes months to disappear. Whilst not a structure as such, the retaining wall is part and parcel of the civil engineering *milieu* and is worth mentioning. The sketch, Fig 12/10 shows one of the many versions to be found alongside the main line. There can be a fair amount of work involved, but on a layout oriented towards operation, no other backcloth is required.

BUILDING AND STRUCTURES

f there is one area on a model railway where scratchbuilding comes fully into its own, it is the buildings. For a start, there are very few kits and even fewer ready-made structures for the British prototype on the market and so, if one relies on these, the resulting model does take on a highly standardized appearance. Apart from this, the choice of prototype is enormous, and as building construction, full sized and model, is based on the concept of interlocked boxes, it is probably the ideal area for the individual to flex his skills at real modelmaking.

Furthermore, model buildings can be made from virtually anything you happen to have to hand. I would not advocate metal, or all that in my youth, tinplate was the accepted medium for all commercial models. The most popular materials are plastic sheet, card, wood and hardboard. Each has its advocates, each has difficulties. For myself, I like plastic sheet, mainly because I don't like working in card. I also use 3 mm ply for larger structures, again because it is a material I find pleasant to work with. However, almost all model buildings are hybrid structures, since one tends to use anything that happens to be around that is suitable for the task.

The structure shown in Fig 13/1 is a brick-built hut of a pattern generally used by coal merchants, but in point of fact, the design is

Fig 13/1 *Exploded diagram showing a simple structure.*

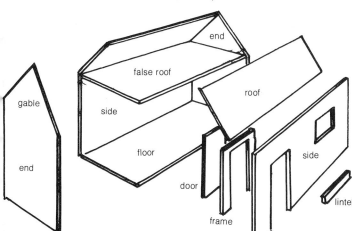

equally applicable to any one of half-a-dozen different buildings tha are to be found around the goods yard. It breaks down into a series of plain walls, plus a small base and a roof, with an optional false roo which serves to keep the structure rigid.

It is rather basic and very simple, and I've deliberately left the surface finish open, as there are many possibilities, ranging from hand painting, individual scribing of bricks, the application of brick paper or the use, at the outset, of embossed plastic sheet to provide the brick effect. This last is the more expensive method, but it is the one I prefer. However, for a first effort, an ideal material is the humble cereal packet. Then when you go wrong, as most of us do a the start, you can follow the approved procedure, which is to put the offending model on the floor and jump on it, violently, thus relieving your feelings. Then make another.

Of course, joining the corners of a card model isn't easy. One good method is to use gummed parcel tape, which, whilst largel superseded by the self-adhesive plastic varieties, can usually be found in a good stationers. You need the narrower variety, which you cut into lengths and fold down the middle, as in Fig 13/2 forming a sharp right angle. The gum is moistened (use a sponge c roller — it tastes awful) and apply to the inside of the structure a shown.

Before you fit the roof, you need to cover the walls in brick pape Here, I'm glad to say, modern adhesives make life easier, as eithe rubber-based adhesive (cow gum) or white glue do not stain th brickpaper, and make life a lot easier. Incidentally, you apply th adhesive to the brickpaper, not the model carcass, and, when it is i place, you take a scalpel or sharp craft knife and carefully cu

Left *A simple hut—a good project for a first attempt at building construction.*

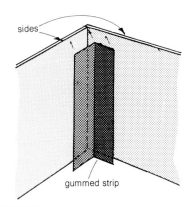

Right Fig 13/2 *Using gummed strip to join card sides.*

Below Fig 13/3 *Folding brickpaper inside door and window openings.*

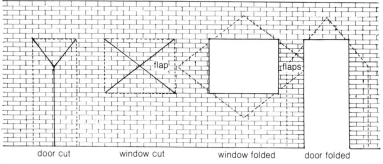

| door cut | window cut | window folded | door folded |

diagonal slits across the window opening and a 'Y'-shaped slit at the door so that the brickpaper may be folded back in the openings, leaving a brick finish to the edge as shown in Fig 13/3.

There is just one small snag with our simple card building, which you will realize if you compare your model with a full sized brick-built hut, the walls are much too thin. As a rough measure, the minimum thickness of a brick wall is 12 in, ie, two rows of brick and an air gap. For very simple structures, a brick built outhouse, for example, the wall may be 3 in thick, ie, a single brick, but there will be 9 in piers every four to six feet, though these may be on the inside. For this reason, it is customary to make good models out of several thicknesses of card or plastic, which allows one to introduce a good deal of relief detail whilst constructing the model.

At this point it's as well to mention that bricks are bonded and that there are three common bonds to be seen, as shown in Fig 13/4. The simple 'garden wall' bond is no longer confined to walls, for with the introduction of cavity wall construction, most buildings have

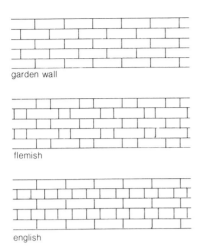

garden wall

flemish

english

Left Fig 13/4 *Brick bonds.*

Below Fig 13/5 *Multi-layer window construction.*

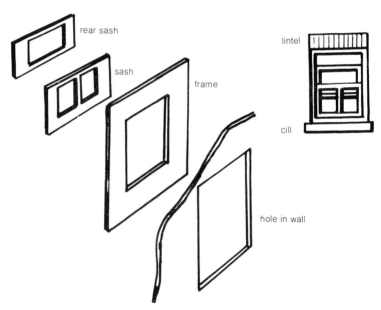

rear sash

sash

frame

lintel

cill

hole in wall

only an outer shell one brick thick, and the simple bond is linked to the inner wall with metal ties. This system of cross bonding appears on modern retaining walls, and is normal on the latest brick cladding for larger buildings. Where a double row of brick is correctly bonded,

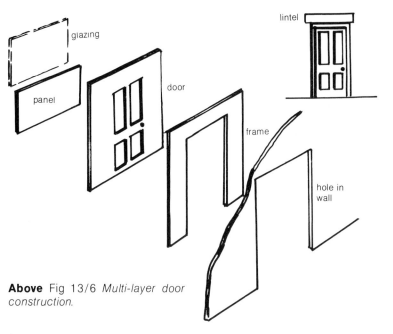

Above Fig 13/6 *Multi-layer door construction.*

the more usual arrangement is the very attractive Flemish bond, where headers and stretchers alternate. The English bond, with alternate rows of headers and stretchers is fairly uncommon, and as a rule, is only to be found on older buildings. Garden wall and Flemish bonds are obtainable in both embossed plastic sheet and brickpapers, but I've not seen any English bond as yet.

You now need some windows. Fig 13/5 shows the basic method, which I advise the outright beginner to follow. To hold the glazing material in place, use a couple of strips of Sellotape, otherwise the darned stuff will only fall out shortly after you've finished the model. Doors are also built up in layers, as shown in Fig 13/6.

The roof is glued in place, bargeboards are added, the roof covered with tile paper and a simple ridge effect added. Finally, the chimney is cut from a piece of wood, covered in brickpaper and stuck in place. The chimney-pot is made from a length of discarded ballpoint pen refil, forced in a drilled hole in the end of the wood.

If you prefer to use embossed plastic sheet, then you will be able to stick the sides together without any special preparation. Use one of the solvents, applied to the inside with a brush, rather than a plastic cement from a tube, it is quicker, neater and doesn't create a

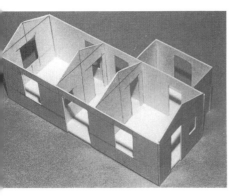

Left *A small station building: the main carcass made from styrene sheet. Note internal partitions provided in prototype positions.*

Below left *The carcass has now been covered in embossed styrene sheet to represent the timber cladding. Further strips of styrene sheet have been attached to form the main timbers, and brick chimneys have been added.*

Bottom *Three miniature lamps are wired in place. As they will be run on half their rated voltage, to give a mellow golden glow and longer life, there is no reason why they cannot be soldered in place.*

Right *The carcass has now been painted, and doors and windows added. All glazing slips into slots in the multi-layer window surrounds.*

Below right *With the addition of a roof, the model is virtually complete. Some posters and station boards will be added. The lamp is made from perspex, a 'grain of wheat' bulb and some copper wire for the bracket.*

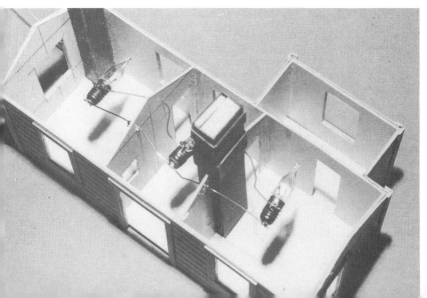

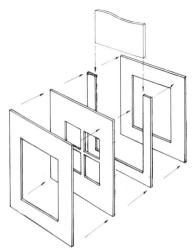

Left Fig 13/7 *Multi-layer window construction incorporating integral glazing.*

Below right *The rear of a low-relief station building, made from styrene sheet.*

Bottom right *The front of a set of low-relief station buildings for a small terminus. The embossed stone styrene sheet provides a pleasing relief effect. A small complete building—in point of fact, the Gents' toilet block—is to the left of the picture.*

mess. The photographs show a small 'timber' station building in various stages of construction. It is constructed entirely from plastic sheet, which provides the surface relief.

The possibilities opened up by multi-layer construction are considerable and the effects are limited only by your own observation of full-sized structures and your willingness to mark out and then cut out the various layers. A useful tip here is that if you make an opening in the outer layer, then pencil around inside, the resulting line will be roughly half a millimetre inside, which works out just about right for an inner wooden lining.

I would, in particular, mention the business of multi-layered windows which are used in the small station building in the photographs. As I mentioned earlier, it is extremely difficult to persuade any transparent material to stop in place inside a model building. Indeed, one of the sub-clauses of Murphy's Law states that model windows fall out shortly after the roof has been glued permanently in place. I prefer, nowadays, to go to the trouble of making windows in layers, as shown in Fig 13/7, so that, at the end, after the window frame has been painted, the glazing can be slid into the slot. It is a lot of work, but the fact that the plastic is held firmly in place and cannot buckle is, in my opinion, worth the extra effort.

A modern all-glass building is best built around a perspex box. As perspex, except in very large sizes, is not that easy to obtain, I suggest that you look in the *Yellow Pages* for firms specializing in commercial display construction. They often use perspex in their work, and will sometimes be prepared to sell offcuts to a fellow craftsman — mention that you are a modelmaker. A more serious snag with perspex is that the recommended adhesive is chloroform. It can be bought from chemists, but once again, you must make it clear that you are a modelmaker, and you will have to sign the poison book. On the whole, all this is a very good reason for not modelling modern buildings, but having said that, I personally, find the varying textures of the infill panels extremely attractive, and anyone modelling in the diesel era needs to give this careful consideration.

Large buildings, and all open buildings — locomotive and goods sheds are classic examples of this type of model — need a very strong structure. For these, I would advocate a ply carcass. The fact that you are then using 3 mm thick material is a help, since the prototype will probably have 24 in thick walls and so your windows will be correctly inset. The fretsaw is an essential tool here.

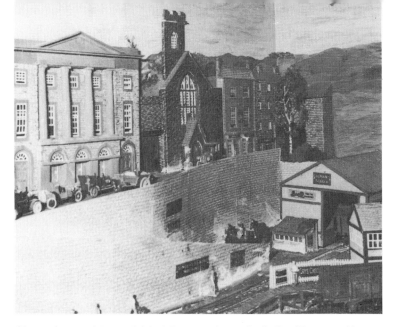

Above *A row of low relief buildings on the author's first 'Tregunna' layout.*

Below *2 mm scale buildings on the Manchester MRS's 'Grandsmoor' layout. Even in this small scale, considerable detail can be included.*

A building is brought to life with the small details. Doorknobs are easily made from pins, downpipes from wire or round plastic rod. Guttering, however, is more difficult. It is possible to score thick plastic sheet to form a gutter, you may find odd lengths of plastic rod of suitable section. If you can find a damaged umbrella with the older pattern 'U'-shaped ribs, you're in luck, for these make excellent model gutters.

So far, we've considered buildings 'in the round', but on a model railway with a backscene, the low-relief structure is deservedly popular. It consists of a facade and a little else — the film set is a good case in point if you want a prototype. The depth can be as little as 4 mm, just sufficient to allow a little relief detail, or as deep as 50 mm — after this, the model becomes more a truncated solid structure. In Fig 13/8 I show the arrangement in section, with (in Fig 13/9) an elevation and plan of a simple arrangement offering a good deal of variation in the depth of the modelled structures. This adds considerably to the realism of the model.

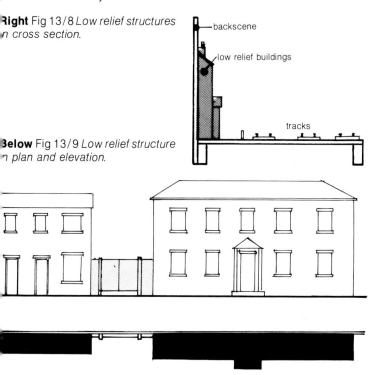

Right Fig 13/8 *Low relief structures in cross section.*

backscene

low relief buildings

tracks

Below Fig 13/9 *Low relief structure in plan and elevation.*

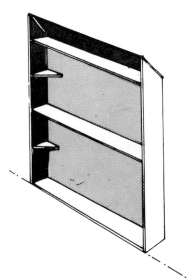

Left Fig 13/10 *Rear view of low relief construction.*

Below *The canal wharf on Peter Denny's 'Buckingham'. This row of industrial buildings is one of the more effective scenic features on a superb example of the model-maker's craft.*

Bottom *This small hut on Dave Lowery's 'Bevleys' layout was constructed from plaster panels made in Linka moulds.*

Right *Part of the late John H. Ahern's Madderport on the 'Madder Valley'. This model was the first to fully exploit the potential of model building construction in connection with a model railway, and despite its age, stands comparison with all but the very best work of the present day.*

Low relief modelling is very simple, and probably the best way to get into modelling structures. Fig 13/10 shows how a model looks from the back, whilst some photographs have been included to show something of the potential. The beauty of low relief modelling lies in the fact that one, naturally, chooses a series of interesting facades, and so the duller parts of the building aren't modelled — resulting in a lovely economy of effort! As, in many cases, very little room is left for buildings on a small baseboard, low relief modelling, which can extend to railway structures, adds to the illusion of depth without using up valuable space.

Certainly, it is a lot easier to model a townscape in low relief than to attempt to paint realistic buildings on a sheet of hardboard. Indeed, some modellers have omitted any real backscene, allowing

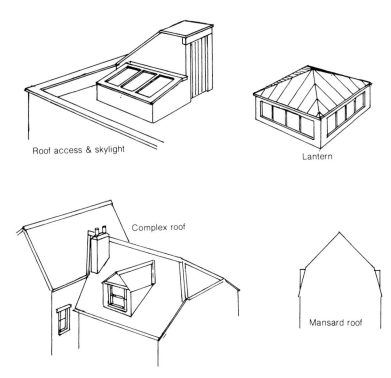

Roof access & skylight

Lantern

Complex roof

Mansard roof

Fig 13/11 *Some examples of interesting roof detail.*

low relief structures to create the illusion that the buildings extend towards infinity. Even a series of thin structures, little more than a building side pasted onto thick card and cut out, gives an illusion of depth, but with this type of model, you must either have a flat roof, or the gable ends must face the viewer. If you want to create the illusion of a sloping roof, the model must be at least 9 mm in depth.

Having mentioned roofs, I will reiterate a point made by many writers — on any model townscape, the roof is very visible. So, not only should you take care to make the roof as accurately as possible, you should seek out prototypes with interesting roofs. This means not only dormers and skylights, some examples of which are shown in Fig 13/11, but flat roofs with gardens, or even swimming pools! The main problem is that prototype roofs, in general, are rather hard to observe, unless you happen to work in a tall office block in the centre of a city.

LOCOMOTIVES AND ROLLING STOCK

A model railway requires locomotives, coaches and wagons — that much is certain for these are the kernel of the layout. They are also, collectively, the part that will cost most, for here, more than anywhere else, there are no cheap and easy short cuts. In the commercially developed scales, OO (and HO for Continental and US prototypes) and N, buying your locomotives and stock in a ready-to-run form is the most economical approach.

An important question is how few locomotives, coaches and wagons does one need to stock an interesting model railway? The short answer is — a lot fewer than you'd think! Indeed, the schemes I've put forward do not require more than three items of motive power, including, in modern idiom, railcar sets, together with two or three coaches, a dozen wagons and, on steam age layouts, a goods brake van. At the outset, much less is adequate.

So, let's start at the beginning. In the initial stages, whilst you are constructing the layout, you need one item of motive power for test

This goods platform on the Macclesfield club's OO gauge layout not only shows the arrangement of the edging flagstones and the stone fascia, but emphasises the fact, often overlooked on models, that in general, platforms are on virtually the same level as the approach road. This could be said to be one of the most important differences between a toy and a model!

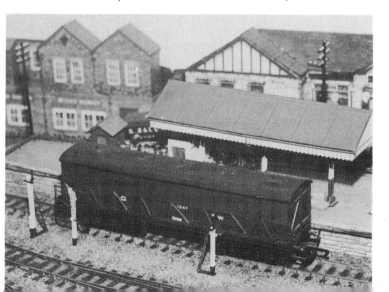

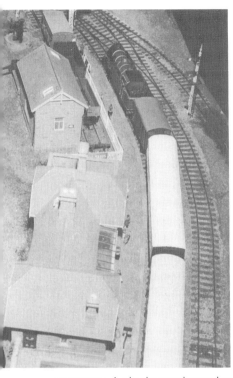

purposes. A single maximum length coach is needed for clearance tests, and an array of odd wagons are handy to prove the most important point, that you can push a train over your pointwork. It's helpful to have, for steam age layouts, an outside-cylindered locomotive to ensure that you have left enough platform clearance at curves. In the initial stages, it is vital to test the track, and to establish that proper working clearances are achieved.

If you are working on a very tight budget and have nothing to hand, then your first item of motive power should be the cheapest working model you can get in your chosen gauge. If it doesn't actually fit into your overall scheme, don't worry at this stage, even if the prototype is horribly wrong for your purpose, it will still test your tracks and, later, can either be 'sold out of service' or, more probably, cannibalized. Rolling stock, on the other hand, ought to be carefully chosen, as it has little second-hand value.

For downright economy, there is nothing to match current British Rail as a prototype, there is so much inexpensive equipment

available and diesels are true mixed traffic machines. The ubiquitous Class '25' BoBo or Class '31' A1A-A1A will make an excellent initial all-round unit, equally at home on passenger or freight trains.

For steam age modelling, the question of prototype choice arises and, with it, the varying selection of ready-to-run items that are currently available. The ideal low-cost period for steam age modelling is the 1950s. MK1 stock had just begun to appear, so you can use the cheapest coaches available. Moreover most of the pre-nationalization classes currently available in ready to run form were still running, and as they are nearly all available in correct BR colours you have no problems at all, whilst the BR designs available widens your choice immensely.

Even in steam days, a stud of five locomotives is ample for an interesting layout whilst the branch line can be correctly operated by just one small tank locomotive.

Where no commercial ready-to-run model exists for a particular

Ex-Cambrian Railways 2-4-0T, built from a GEM kit, painted in undercoat. A simple kit for a beginner.

prototype, the modeller must rely on his own resources. Further-more, only in 4 mm scale is there anything like an extensive selection of kits on offer. Thus scratchbuilding will be very much a fact of life for anyone wanting to move into historical modelling of the steam age, or who wants to work in anything but 4 mm scale

Scratchbuilding is not really difficult. After all, it isn't that long since we had little option but to build models from basic raw materials and a handful of components. Many kits by contrast are not that easy to assemble, and the difficulties are frequently compounded by indifferent instructions, which with just a few honourable exceptions, range from the inadequate to the abysmal The worst can be quickly summed up in one short sentence; 'Put the bits together'.

Kits come in three main categories, plastic, cast whitemetal and etched brass. In the main, plastic kits are confined to coaches (a few) and wagons. Most loco kits are made from cast whitemetal often with etched parts added. These kits do not fall together and, in extreme cases, it would probably be as easy to scratchbuild the model. The etched brass kit is relatively new. Some are excellent, a few are indifferent to poor, but all are, apart from the matter of cost, rather easier than scratchbuilding, and provide full rivet or panelling detail. When properly assembled, and correctly painted, they produce superb models.

However, if cost is a major consideration, then you should turn to scratchbuilding. I would suggest that in such cases, it might be advisable to consider either TT gauge, or 7 mm scale. The point is that in TT you are not, generally, expected to reach high standards, and you aren't competing with commercial products either, whilst in 7 mm scale, you're handling much larger parts.

There is a general belief that O gauge is only for the very rich, but I've known quite a few modellers who turned to this scale solely because their funds were stretched and they found they went further in the largest scale. The larger scale is definitely easier for

Peter Denny's scratchbuilt 'Sacre' 2-4-0T Altrincham Tank shows what can be done with a relatively simple toolkit (positively no machine tools) and, of course, a good deal of determination.

the home constructor, and, furthermore you don't need a lot of stock to make a very good impression.

There is absolutely no reason why you should scratchbuild in metal for many model locomotives have been built from plastic sheet and, providing the finished model is properly ballasted with lead and is neatly painted, it's impossible to tell the difference without picking it up and inspecting the underneath. Indeed, if you want to scratchbuild a diesel or electric locomotive then plastic sheet, with a little wood reinforcement, is the preferred material.

Coaches are generally scratchbuilt from wood, card or plastic sheet. If anything, a good model of a coach, particularly a panelled coach, is rather more difficult than a straightforward steam locomotive, and far more trouble than a diesel loco! As a result, if a commercial plastic coach of roughly the same style exists, modellers today prefer to cut, carve and re-assemble the body shells to suit. This is particularly so in the case of modern BR stock, for although all the BR coach groups have been produced in 4 mm scale, only in the case of the rather standardized Mk III is there anything like a comprehensive coverage, whilst the paucity of diesel railcars is notorious. However, as BR conveniently uses a standard profile and standard window and door openings, the keen modeller can have a lot of innocent fun cutting and carving relatively inexpensive items in order to produce the desired model. It's worth pointing out that the coach bogies can frequently be obtained as spares — this is very useful for Mk I stock, which ran on three different types of bogie. You can often find slightly damaged coaches on scale at exhibitions very cheaply indeed. Clearly, if you're going to hack it about, do a few broken bits matter?

BIBLIOGRAPHY

Note This is a selective bibliography, and is divided into two parts; the first — books which should be readily available; the second — a few classics which are not easy to lay your hands on, but which are well worth hunting down. Ideally, reference books should be bought and kept on your own bookshelves, since you will need to have them to hand. However, initially you may need to go to your local public library, where the staff can arrange to get the books on loan if they are not on the shelves. The catch is that postage is so high today, it will not cost a great deal more to buy them.

I should also mention the existence of specialist libraries. The best is to be found at Keen House, the HQ of the Model Railway Club but is available only to members of that body. Every one of the books I mention is to be found within this definitive collection, together with most English language model and prototype magazines and a vast collection of books on all aspects of the prototype. Unfortunately one needs to live or work in London to make full use of the MRC library. The Manchester MRS too has an extremely good library and also holds a very detailed index to magazines.

Books in print

Buckingham, Great Central, Peter Denny (Peco). This account of the construction and development of one of the finest model railways ever built contains an invaluable glossary of hints and tips culled from a lifetime's modelling. As the layout was definitely built on a budget, the advice is of enormous value, and the photographs show just how much can be done on a modest weekly outlay.

Model railroading with John Allen, Linn Westcott (Kalmbach). Forget the fact that this is about an American layout. John Allen's 'Gorre and Daphetid' (pronounced 'gory and defeated', mispronounced several dozen incorrect ways) is an inspiration to anyone interested in the hobby. It is lavishly illustrated, with masses of superb colour, and as the layout grew from a very small 6 ft × 4 ft model is an example of just what one can do by plain determination, even though the builder, discovering that work was interfering with modelmaking, opted for a very early retirement!

Model Locomotive Construction, Guy Williams (Ian Allan). This is probably the best current work on the subject, though it is advisable to stress that the author, who builds models for Pendon Museum, works to very exacting standards and aims for the highest quality. However, it is best to aim high and falter a little than to aim low — and still miss!

Building Model Locomotives, F.J. Roche & G.C. Templar (Ian Allan). This is an edited reprint of a long series of articles in *Model Railway Constructor* during the 1950s, and is mainly oriented towards O gauge. Again it aims at a very high standard of modelmaking.

Buildings for Model Railways, Maurice H. Bradley (David & Charles). An excellent all round handbook on building construction by a talented modelmaker and professional architect.

Modelled Architecture, Dave Rowe (Wild Swan). Dave Rowe's modelled landscapes with a little railway interest are well known on the exhibition circuit, and in this excellent handbook, he shows how he goes about constructing his models. The book is relatively inexpensive and thus of particular value.

Period Railway Modelling: Buildings, Vivien Thompson (Peco). This book deals with the construction of buildings from plastic card, and provides a wealth of information on the use of this material.

Practical Electronics for Railway Modellers (2 vols), Roger Amos (Patrick Stephens). Easily the best, and most practical books on ths complex subject.

Scenic Railway Modelling, edited by Michael Andress (Patrick Stephens). An interesting compilation of short, wholly practical essays on various aspects of small scale scenic modelling by various modelmakers. It is important to bear in mind that individual techniques differ in detail, and therefore, when following the excellent ideas, beware of crossing the methods. It may work, but on the other hand, it might well lead to serious difficulties.

Modelling Historic Railways, David Jenkinson (Patrick Stephens). This book is primarily concerned with prototype research and is based firmly on the author's own work on the Settle & Carlisle Railway. As a result, it is crammed with incidental information on this line in particular, and the Midland Railway and LMS (Midland Division) in general. The principles described are equally applicable should one be interested in current practice.

Out of print books

Miniature Building Construction, Miniature Locomotive Construction and *Miniature Landscape Modelling,* J.H. Ahern. These three textbooks date from the late '40s and early '50s, but the basic principles remain more or less unaltered. Some materials are difficult, if not impossible to obtain, but modern equivalents are superior anyway.

Indoor Model Railways, E.W. Twining. This pre-war book, by a pioneer modelmaker, contains a little useful practical information and a mass of scenic inspiration.

Railway Modelling in Miniature, Edward Beal. Edward Beal's first book and in many ways, his best and most enduring work. Revised several times, it enshrines the standard practice in 4 mm scale during the 1930s (Teddy Beal practically launched the OO-HO field) and is full of useful ideas. Pity that pins in paper no longer exist!

The Craft of Modelling Railways, Edward Beal. Not so much a practical textbook as a broad account of the hobby in the late '30s, Teddy Beal's second book makes delightful reading to this day. The advertisements at the back are interesting, providing you remember that, in 1938, anyone earning over £5 a week was very well off indeed.

Model Railways, Henry Greenly. Although published in 1924, this book owes more to pre-WW1 practice. However, there are many useful ideas to be gleaned, and, in particular, Greenly's designs for railway structures are of considerable value. He had a wonderful knack for creating an authentic looking model which, whilst far from being true to scale, appeared to be correct. This was invaluable when it was necessary to cut a large station building or goods shed down to a size to fit onto the inevitably undersized model railway baseboard.

INDEX